The Logic of God

God

A Divine Cosmic Joke

Written Through
Robert Keegan
Created, Directed and Produced by
Consciousness

Order this book online at www.trafford.com/07-2528
or email orders@trafford.com

Most Trafford titles are also available at major online book retailers.

Note for Librarians: A cataloguing record for this book is available from Library
and Archives Canada at www.collectionscanada.ca/amicus/index-e.html

Printed in Victoria, BC, Canada.

ISBN: 978-1-4251-5640-4

*We at Trafford believe that it is the responsibility of us all, as both individuals
and corporations, to make choices that are environmentally and socially sound.
You, in turn, are supporting this responsible conduct each time you purchase a
Trafford book, or make use of our publishing services. To find out how you are
helping, please visit www.trafford.com/responsiblepublishing.html*

*Our mission is to efficiently provide the world's finest, most comprehensive
book publishing service, enabling every author to experience success.
To find out how to publish your book, your way, and have it available
worldwide, visit us online at www.trafford.com/10510*

 www.trafford.com

North America & international
toll-free: 1 888 232 4444 (USA & Canada)
phone: 250 383 6864 ♦ fax: 250 383 6804 ♦ email: info@trafford.com

The United Kingdom & Europe
phone: +44 (0)1865 722 113 ♦ local rate: 0845 230 9601
facsimile: +44 (0)1865 722 868 ♦ email: info.uk@trafford.com

10 9 8 7 6 5 4

Warning!
This book may be offensive to some viewers.
If you find yourself yawning or saying bull feces more than once
while reading Part One, perhaps you will enjoy laughing
at Part Two, or maybe not.
Either way…Que Sera Sera

Preface

Perhaps you are wondering why this book is not signed per se, as 'written by' an author, as books usually are?

Is he modest? Is it pride? Is it humility? Or cleverness?

Here are a few words from a book titled "Fingers Pointing Toward The Moon".

This book was one of eight written through and entified with the signature of Wei Wu Wei (which roughly translated means spontaneous, non-volitional action), and may be an appropriate explanation.

"What is a name? Is it not the symbol of someone who regards himself as a separate individual? Is not a name essentially - the name of an ego? But the Self, the Principal, the I-Reality has no name. 'The Tao that can be named is not the real Tao'. One of the greatest books in the world opens with those words.

Tom, Dick, and Harry think that they have written the books that they signed, or painted the pictures, composed the music, built the churches. But they exaggerate. It was a pen that did it, or some other implement. They held the pen? Yes, but the hand that held the pen was an implement too, as is the brain that controlled the hand. They were intermediaries, instruments, just apparatus. Even the best apparatus does not need a personal name like Tom, Dick, or Harry.

If the nameless builders of the Taj Mahal, of Chartres, of Rheims, of a hundred cathedral symphonies, knew that – and avoided the solecism of attributing to their own egos the works that were created through their instrumentality – may not even a jotter-down of passing metaphysical notions know it also.

If you should not understand this – give the book away before reading it! But give it to a pilgrim on the Way. Why? Because it would have helped the pilgrim that compiled it, if it had been given to him. And that is why he compiled it, and why he presumes to offer it to other pilgrims."

W.W.W.

Contents

Warning 5

Preface 7

Context 13

Credits 15

Introduction 17

Dedication 19

Robert's search 21

The Bottom Line 23

The Understanding 25

Understanding vs.
Faith and Belief 27

Reason vs. Truth 29

Consciousness is all there is 31

What is a human being really? 33

Bestowing of Endowment 35

Ego – the Great Pretender 37

The BMO computer 39

Programming (conditioning) 41

The CIA vs. True Intelligence 43

Don't take it personally! 45

How does God function? 47

Free Will 49

Divine Hypnosis 51

Cosmic Law 53

(Sh)it happens 55

The end of pride and guilt 57

The end of jealousy, envy
and hate 59

The Unforgiven Sin 61

The end of worry and
disappointment 63

Freedom—Do whatever you
want to do 65

The Devil made me do it! 67

Planning for Now 69

The 'why' question 71

Calling and Purpose 73

A Universal Problem 75

Out of the wild blue yonder 77

Contemplating Meditation 79

Prayer 81

Is God a vegetarian? 83

Marvellous Diversity 85

Gandhi vs. Bush 87

Co-creation makes sense 89

Personal un-development 91

The I of the i — insight, instinct,
intuition and intention 93

Life – a synchronistic,
circumstantial, accidental
coincidence 95

A Divine Play 99

Theatre of the Absurd 101

Happy Days 103

Me, myself and Irene 105

Miracle on 34th Street 107

Groundhog Day 109

The Meaning of Life 111

Death of a Salesman 113

Karma and the Academy Awards 115

I Love Lucy 117

From Here to Eternity 119

Mr. Destiny 121

Heaven Can Wait 123

Soul Train 125

Sex and the City 127

War of the Roses 129

Romancing the Stone 131

The Passion of Christ 135

Married with Children 137

Anger Management 139

Fear Factor 141

The Good the Bad and the Ugly 143

A Kodak Moment 145

Houston, we have a problem… Uh-oh, better call Maaco! 147

Gone With the Wind 149

Forest Gump 151

As Good As It Gets 153

The Magoo Factor 155

To Kill a Mockingbird 157

The Legend of Bagger Vance 159

Shell's Wonderful World of Golf 161

The Accidental Tourist 163

Analyze this! 165

Bruce Almighty 167

Back to the Future 169

Mr. Ed 171

An Inconvenient Truth 173

Hero 175

What the Bleep do we know?! 177

City Slickers 179

The secret of 'The Secret' 181

Pulp Fiction 183

Ebony and Ivory 185

"I am what I am."—Popeye 187

The Heart of Rock 'n Roll is still beating! 189

That's a Wrap 191

The Final Curtain 193

Elvis has left the building 195

The Ultimate Understanding— There is nothing happening! 197

The Matrix vs. The Ultimate Understanding 199

Unicity 201

Major Contributions to Robert's Search for Truth 207

Courses, Seminars and Coaching 215

The Three Mysticeers 217

Context

Most of the concepts presented evolved through the teaching of three of the world's greatest *living sages – Ramesh S. Balsekar, David R. Hawkins, and Eckhart Tolle.

They have contributed immensely to the recontextualizing and understanding of Consciousness or God.

Eckhart, through his best selling, "The Power of NOW" and "Stillness Speaks".

David through his work in, "Power vs. Force", "The Eye of the I", and "I".

And Ramesh, through his teaching in, "Consciousness Speaks", and "Who Cares?!"

There is deep and enormous gratitude for the simple yet profound understanding that happened through his Unicity teachings.

His (Ramesh's) words are woven throughout the fabric of this book, and his message makes up the context…

Consciousness is…all there is.

* (As of 07/07/07 - See page 217 for biographies).

Credits

This book could not have been written without input through the following.
And many, many others (see major contributions pg 207 - pg 213).

Paul Anka
Marcus Aurelius
Buddha
Rhett Butler
Curly
Lieutenant Columbo
Fred Couples
Dad
Roger Ebert
Mr. Ed
Meister Eckhart
Forest Gump
Jesus
Brian Klemmer
Wayne Liquorman
Biff Loman
J. Krishnamurti
Nisargatta Maharaj
Ramana Maharshi
Paul McCartney
Mom
Jack Nicklaus
Jack Nicholson
Popeye
Monte Python
Ricky Ricardo
Rumi
Wei Wu Wei
Tiger Woods

Introduction

Coming from a business background, I always thought that in order to be successful in life; logic, or things making sense was a mandatory requirement.

This thinking is the core of this book.

And, a little humour also helps!

Dedication

This book is dedicated to the KISS principle.

Robert's search

I had what society might consider a successful life.

I had a successful business.

I had a successful family.

I had a lot of successful friends.

But I seemed to be always searching for more. There was a constant underlying unease.

I was a personal development/self-improvement junky.

And once I cashed-in the successful business, bought two his and hers silver Mercedes and the big house, the searching seamed to intensify.

This searching then turned inward and led to an even loftier goal, Self-realization or 'Enlightenment'!

I saw Enlightenment as the only way to finally put an end to this incessant search. And I set about finding It with the same enthusiasm that I had used to build my successful life.

However, It continued to elude me.

Perhaps the searching was just to understand or find meaning for what was motivating the searching.

Then one day I made a discovery. Or rather, *a discovery was made.*

The discovery was that it was not me that was searching, but that Consciousness was seeking Itself… what a relief!

This 'understanding' has brought with it not only a sense of relief, but also a sense of freedom that is hard to convey in words.

The understanding is that *no one is making anything happen.* And, that Bob is but a programmed instrument of the Source, and simply cannot do anything that he is not programmed to do.

I finally understand and accept that Enlightenment may or may not *happen* in this lifetime and that I cannot *do* anything to make it happen.

For me, getting comfortable with not knowing what might happen next was/is truly liberating and brings more wonder and adventure into life, and more Life to the present moment!

And, besides, *"What if this is as good as it gets?"*

The Bottom Line

"Events happen, deeds are done, but there is no individual doer thereof."

— Buddha

The Understanding

1. Consciousness—Source, or God, or Primal Energy—is all there is.

2. There is only *one* Source.

3. From this one Source all phenomenon of form was/is created.

4. The human being is but one of the billions of created form objects.

5. The human being has been created and programmed by the Source.

6. Only the Source can create because It is the Master Programmer.

7. Therefore, the human being is really a programmed instrument or object. Ramesh calls it a body/mind organism. Let's call it a bmo for short.

8. An object (bmo) can only do what it is programmed to do.

9. Therefore, the human being *is not the author* of any doing.

10. So, whatever the human being does or doesn't do is the will of the Source.

11. Therefore, whatever the body/mind organism does is 'ok' because it is the will of the Source or God or Primal Energy or Cosmic Law.

12. And, any consequences that arise from the doing are also God's will.

13. Things may happen (arise) but I am not the 'doer'.

14. Therefore, I am free to do whatever I want because I am only an instrument of the Source…and, any consequences that may arise are also part of the Program.

Understanding vs. Faith and Belief

Faith is defined in the dictionary as; "complete confidence or *belief* in something without objective proof (like Santa Claus)".

Faith often relates to a particular system of religious beliefs.

Beliefs tend to perhaps keep the mind closed to new information.

To understand is to grasp the meaning or to interpret something in one of a number of possible ways. Because all language is subjective and can only be conceptual, what someone understands by words may not be what is meant by the speaker or writer.

Understanding is completely different and is defined in the dictionary as; "the power to make experience intelligible by applying concepts. Having intelligence or insight."

However, understanding doesn't proceed simply from examining data; it comes from examining data and applying concepts in a particular context.

And, the context of 'the understanding' is—Consciousness is all there is

Understanding *happens*. It is like a flash of insight from 'out of the blue'. When it comes to understanding there is no room for doubt, only a deep knowing that something is true.

Reason vs. Truth

Perhaps this book will appeal more to those bmo's who are functioning in the calibration level of the 400's—Reason or Logic. Anyone who has read Dr. David R. Hawkins' books will understand what is meant by calibrated levels of consciousness.

The proposition that is presented in his book *"Power vs. Force",* is that the human mind is like a computer terminal connected to a giant database. And that all life emanates an invisible energy within the all-encompassing field of Consciousness itself, which is primordial to life.

According to Dr. Hawkins research, each human organism has a programmed level of Consciousness (or Life energy) that can be measured, And after a twenty nine year study, he along with Linus Pauling, came up with "The Map of Consciousness".

This discovery is said to be *'the wormhole'* between the concepts of the linear Newtonian world of measurement (time/space, subject/object) and the non-linear world of Quantum Physics, Non-Linear Dynamics, Chaos Theory and Oneness

The "Map"—a logarithmic scale of levels of this Life energy—is from 1 to 1000.

Where "1" represents the lowest level of consciousness of life (bacteria), and "1,000" the highest level sustained by humans (the Big Guys—Christ, Buddha, Krishna).

The scale also represents the level of Truth and perception. Consciousness level of the 400's is where Science and the intellect live. This is the level of the greatest human minds, i.e.: Newton, Einstein and Freud. They all calibrated at 499.

The 500's is the beginning of a paradigm shift from the dimension of thought and form to the formless, the level of Love. The great power of the 500's is in the use of the faculty of understanding, and it is understanding that allows for the progression to 540, the level of Unconditional Love and on up to Peace and Enlightenment at level 600. Of course, nothing happens unless it has been written into the Program.

However, perhaps the logical or intellectual understanding of *the Understanding,* might facilitate the minds' acceptance of the concepts presented here. Or maybe not.

Consciousness is all there is

Consciousness—Source, God, Tao, Truth, The Way, Mind, The Great Mystery, The Unnameable, Primal or Universal Energy, Cosmic Law or Love – is all there is.

All there is, is Consciousness.

We/you/I are mere objects projected in space.

Space and time are concepts, a mechanism for objects to be extended.

For three-dimensional objects to be extended, the concept of space is necessary.

And, the concept of time is necessary for objects to be observed.

Unless an object is observed, it doesn't exist.

I am but an instrument of observation.

So, space and time are merely concepts, a mechanism, created for this manifestation of form to take place. It's amazing how in the last few years, comparatively, science says the same thing.

Everything in the Universe is based on opposites. Nothing in the universe is static. The universe is moving all the time. The universe is always changing from one opposite to another.

However, the opposites are interconnected. They are interrelated polarities. One cannot exist without the other. The changing from one opposite into the other is the very basis of life and existence.

The human being, failing to see the inherent polarity in life, has a feeling of having some kind of control or choice. And perhaps a sense of 'personal' responsibility.

One feels he can exercise his volition and yet, deep down, he knows there is an order infinitely more powerful which seems to dictate his life.

One has the deep feeling, a deep intuitive feeling that one's choices are merely superficial, and his life is actually being lived by a totally different power. An infinitely more powerful principle. A universal Consciousness, before which the individual consciousness is like a candle compared to the sun.

The metaphysical aspects of this understanding are astonishing!

What is a human being really?

When we talk of 'me', we are usually talking of the 'body' which appears to be so solid, but isn't.

As seen through an electron-scanning microscope, the body appears as nothing but emptiness, certainly not a solid object.

Furthermore, the sub-atomic physicist tells us that deep within this emptiness is a nucleus which, being an oscillating field begins to dissolve, showing further organized fields—protons, neutrons and even smaller particles, each of which also dissolve into nothing but the rhythm of the universal pulse.

In other words there is no solidity at all, either at the most sublime level of the body or at the heart of the universe. The compact nucleus at the very heart of the atom, then, is nothing at all but rather a dynamic individual pattern of concentrated energy throbbing and vibrating at an incredible speed.

Basically an individual is really an individual pattern of vibrating energy.

Isn't that interesting?

Bestowing of Endowment

The human being is endowed with sentience.

Like any other animal, sentience allows the senses to work.

The human being is essentially an object plus sentience (just like any other animal or insect), which has the sense of being present, the sense of presence.

Unlike any other animal, the human being has been bestowed with intellect.

Intellect is what allows the human being to interpret and discriminate what is cognized.

So, it is the power of this intellect to discriminate and interpret what is cognized that gives the individual being a sense of individuality and makes him *think* he is something special in this world of billions of form objects.

The body/mind organism I consider myself to be, when conceived, was stamped with certain characteristics: physical, mental, moral, temperamental…so that the Source or Consciousness could produce through that organism certain acts during its lifetime, the period between birth and death.

Ego – the Great Pretender

This *'Logic of God'* concept (and all words are concepts) is: a human being is an object, uniquely programmed by the Source.

Consciousness is 'the impersonal awareness of being'.

The awareness that I have is simply a feeling or sense of being alive. The sense or 'I am' feeling.

So the Source has identified itself with each human object and created this impersonal awareness and immediately identified it with an individual entity.

So this identification, "ego" or small 'm' mind, has been created by the Source.

The word (concept) "ego" has been much maligned.

Notionally, it could be said that the ego/mind is made up of two parts—the ego/thinking mind or intellect, and as Ramesh calls it, the ego/working mind or identified operating element.

The egoic thinking mind/intellect comes in and takes credit for all my thoughts, feelings and actions and pretends that I am a separate independent doer.

It pretends that I have control over my life and in order to stay alive the ego is continuously cycling between memory and imagination or anticipation of the next thing. It worries about the future, specifically its future.

The present moment spells death for the great pretender.

So, the question is, "Is the ego real?"

Well, yes and no. If one notionally thinks of the conceptual ego as a shadow, then one could see that yes, a shadow is both real and unreal.

The BMO computer

So, when I use a computer, what do I do?

I put in the input, then press a button and the output that comes out has nothing to do with the computer's choice. It is strictly according to the programming. Isn't that so?

The computer has no ego to say it is 'my' action.

But this computer, the body/mind organism (bmo) has an ego.

So, the output is strictly according to the programming. The brain reacts to an input over which I have no control, an input that is sent by the Source.

So, the question is, what is this input?

Mostly it is thought. I have a thought which leads to an action, which I say is 'my' action. Now, that next thought that I am going to get, I have no control over, do I?

It has been proven in laboratory experiments that the next thought that we get will happen a split second before we react to that thought and decide to do something or not; the thought arises a split second before we can react to it.

Therefore, I have absolutely no control over the input of thought.

So, one has no control over the input, one has no control over the programming, and yet one says that the output is 'my' decision.

Isn't that interesting?

Programming (conditioning)

"Most people really can't help but be the way they are, as they are being run by innumerable programs which they are not aware of."—David R. Hawkins

I had no choice in being born to particular parents, therefore I had no choice about genes—the unique DNA in this particular human object. This particular human object has a distinct DNA in which even twins are unique.

So one has no choice about genes, about the environment, parents, culture or where geographically one is born.

The genes or DNA plus the environmental conditioning, which includes education, television, newspapers. And social conditioning by parents, peer groups, religious and political leaders. This programming is changing every moment.

Therefore, who I am, the persona or personality, is nothing more than this programming and the sum total of 'my' experiences up to the present moment.

So, at any moment, the persona is an individual entity which had no control over its genes, environment or social conditioning.

Therefore, the persona 'me' is a *fiction,* another concept.

There is truly no 'person' except the feeling of being an independent entity, which has been imposed on the impersonal awareness of being and called the 'ego'.

Robert Keegan is a fiction made up of a bmo and the up-to-the-moment programming. Programming sent by the Source.

Robert does nothing! But, the ego identifies with and takes credit for the incoming thoughts as Bob's/my thoughts. Thoughts, that lead to 'my' action.

However, I now understand that all programming and thoughts emanate from the One Source. Therefore, Bob could not be the author or architect of any doing that comes from those thoughts.

Bob does nothing! Bob is a concept. Bob is a fictional character.

The CIA vs. True Intelligence

The Central *Intellectual* Agency is an aspect of the ego concept.

It orchestrates, copies, sorts, stores and retrieves information.

In addition it evaluates and weighs options and categorizes those options according to their usefulness or gain to 'me'.

To do this it requires abstractions, concepts, symbols, hierarchies of meanings and perceived value, prioritization and selection.

This is made even more effective by constant acquisition of facts and their realignment into modified strata of meaning and significance to 'me'.

Its overriding motivation is to seek pleasure and survival and avoid that which lacks pleasure or is painful to 'me'.

This CIA could be likened to the hardware of a computer. And, might I add, one heck of an impressive processor!

The central processing system of this computer is the brain.

Just like the computer, the brain is but inert matter.

The brain, like the computer runs on input from outside programming.

And, the brain, just like a computer cannot create thoughts.

All it can do is process the incoming data.

True intelligence

Science tells us that the body is made up of approximately 60 trillion cells. Those 60 trillion cells are each doing 6 trillion things per second.

Therefore, there are over 360 trillion things per second happening within the body—new cells created, growth and death of old cells and of course breathing and all the other bodily functions.

The intellect/ego could not possibly control even a small portion of this activity!

Don't take it personally!

So, our respiratory process, our digestion process, our most complicated nervous system—they all work by themselves—it doesn't take a 'me' to control it.

The senses—seeing, hearing, smelling, tasting and touching are 'impersonal'.

Consciousness is seeing through the eyes, hearing through the ears, tasting through the tongue, smelling through the nose and feeling through the touch.

And all the 'normal' bodily functions of eating, sleeping, defecating etc. are actually autonomous and are occurring on their own without a 'me'.

The original sense of presence is also impersonal. When one gets up in the morning the first sense of presence is impersonal. Then it dawns on 'me' that I am so and so. The personal identification comes later.

So, the question is, who is this so and so?

Apart from the body, the 'me' that I think of is but a collection of memories. A collection or collage of impressions, which I myself have about 'me', and which others have about 'me'. The impressions that I have may or may not be a little more flattering than the impressions of others.

Other than a collection of memories and impressions, what is the 'me'?

The 'me' is a self-made image, an illusion, a concept.

All experience is impersonal.

There is no 'personal' experience. Experiences happen through this bmo only in the Present Moment. Then a split second later the mind/ego claims it as 'mine' and says that was a lovely experience or compares it with similar experiences to judge whether or not this one is good or bad.

I am but an object.

There is no difference between any objects in this world. What I *think* is the subject 'myself' is really an object perceived by another object, who himself thinks he is the subject.

Basically, both the observed and the observer are objects.

All objects are merely temporary appearances in Consciousness.

How does God function?

This BMO computer has an operating element which is perhaps similar to the *motherboard* on a conventional computer. This motherboard is the identified consciousness that functions in the body. And, it controls all bodily functions and actions through the chakra and acupuncture systems. This operating element is what some call the spirit body or etheric body. And, some very sensitive human organisms see this etheric body as auras around physical bodies.

The bmo could also be described as a psychosomatic apparatus.

The operating element of this apparatus functions without the sense of 'me' as a doer!

For instance, when one is driving a car on the highway, between certain distances, the 'me' is quite often hardly present. One arrives and then one suddenly realizes they have arrived. But, the one who was driving was the operating element or functioning element.

What was absent was the identification of the operating element as the 'me'.

Perhaps we are like children playing in an amusement park steering toy cars. They are serious, they *think* they are driving. What's more they are supposed to think they are driving. They are entertained because they think they are driving. It wouldn't be any fun otherwise.

Conversely, when one is driving a car on the road, one *thinks* he is driving. But, at a real moment of crisis, is one really in control of the car or does the car 'get' controlled?

Consciousness is all there is.

And, Consciousness is always in the driver's seat!

Free Will

To rub home the primacy of Divine Will, let us juxtapose Mother Teresa with a psychopath. 'Good' things happen through Mother Teresa and 'bad' things happen through a psychopath, because that is how their body/mind organisms have been programmed—neither had any choice.

Essentially, basically each one of us is an object. One forgets that. One forgets that he is an object because the Source has created that object with such a design, let us say 'nature', that the object considers itself a separate entity with volition.

"I have free will. I can do what I like. I'm responsible for my actions. Therefore I can either do good actions or bad actions. I can be brave or timid. I can be kind or I may be unkind. Everything is in my control. I'm in charge of my life."

So, for one who thinks in terms of 'I am in charge of my life', the question is, who is this 'I or my' one is talking about?

The point is that all one is is basically an object. One kind of object. One type of object. One specifically designed and programmed object, but nonetheless an object.

In other words, one is either the Subject, pure Subjectivity, Potentiality, Energy, God, whatever we choose to call it—the Source—the One Reality from which the entire manifestation has come, or one is a created object.

So, there is only pure subjectivity, pure reality, the one Source, which is the subject, the pure subject, and everybody else is an object.

And yet, this is the basic simple truth which everybody forgets. "I want this. I like you. I don't like…etc."

Therefore, the question is: Who is it that wants something? Who does not want something; who likes something, who doesn't like? Who is this?

It is basically an object, isn't that so?

So, if that object is able to *think* that it has volition, then that ability to think that it has volition and is in charge of its life, that itself must have come from the Source.

Can you imagine what would happen if God allowed 6 or 7 billion human organisms to have free will? He would not be able to run the universe with any kind of precision!

Divine Hypnosis

"In the human mechanism, there is a mechanism that prevents the human mechanism from seeing its mechanistic nature." — Ramesh Balsekar

So, when the Source created this human object (bmo), and the parents gave it a name, then by what Ramesh calls Divine Hypnosis, a fiction was also created.

A fiction, that one is an individual entity.

A fiction creating a conceptual identification with a particular body/mind organism and a name—basically a name given to a human object over which I had no control of the programming.

So, I say I make a decision. A decision, which is said to be 'my' decision. But is it really 'my' decision? On what is that decision based?

That decision which one says is 'my' decision is based on genes and environmental up-to-date conditioning and programming.

So the conditioning is going on all the time, and whatever decision I *think* I make is really based on the genes plus the up-to-date programming—the latest television, newspaper or books that have been read, etc. etc.

Isn't that interesting?

So, every decision is based entirely on something over which one has no control. And, the decision 'I' *think* 'I' am making is exactly the decision that Consciousness has programmed me to make.

Cosmic Law

Therefore, on analysis, what one finds is that every decision through a particular body/mind organism is exactly the decision that Source wants/needs to make.

Every decision has been programmed by Consciousness .

And, the subsequent happenings from that decision, is also God's will or the will of the Source.

Jesus said: *"Thy Will be done."*

Because *Thy* (Source) has done the programming.

God is putting in the input.

The output therefore has to be according to God's will.

Thy Will be done. Why?

Because it is according to Cosmic Law that: first, the object is born; second, in that object, the genes and the conditioning have been and continue to be created by the Source.

Therefore, the output has to be according to Cosmic Law. Every single output through every single human computer, every single moment at every single place, has to be the will of the Source.

So, by accepting this, then *nothing can happen* unless it is according to Cosmic Law or the will of God or the Source.

(Sh)it happens

"Considering the endless list of factors required for anything to happen, one can only admit that everything is responsible for everything, however remote. Doership is a myth born from the illusion of 'me' and 'mine'." —Nisargadatta Maharaj

So, events happen, deeds are done, but there is no individual doer thereof.

Which means that any action which one *thinks* is 'mine' or 'yours' or 'his' or 'hers', is not really anyone's action.

Nobody has done anything, but, it has been created. It has happened because it is the will of God or the Source.

And, when this is accepted, what is the result?

Then, it would be silly to blame anyone for any action, wouldn't it?

So, if one is truly able to accept that there is no individual doer (even that is God's will). If one is able to accept that God's will is all there is, nothing can happen unless it is His will.

And therefore, if anything has happened which the human being, or society considers good or evil, it could not have happened unless it was the will of God or the Source.

And, whatever has happened, if it has not been 'done' by anyone, I cannot blame anybody.

By accepting that nothing can happen unless it is the will of God, means that I cease to blame myself or anyone else for what happens.

The terms 'right' or 'wrong' become meaningless!

The end of pride and guilt

When something 'happens' through this bmo that society deems as good and I am rewarded or praised, pleasure may or may not arise—however, knowing that I am not the doer—pride does not arise.

When something 'happens' through this bmo that society deems as bad and I am chastised or punished, regret may or may not arise—however, knowing I am not the doer—guilt and shame do not arise.

There is truly no 'one' to be guilty of anything.

And certainly no shame!

All bmo's are innocent.

There is no such thing as personal responsibility!

I am but an instrument through which life *happens.*

Consciousness is all there is.

The end of jealousy, envy and hate

When one has the understanding that the human being is simply a unique programmed body/mind organism, then one recognizes that there is no *one* 'doing' anything.

And, that everything that happens arises from Consciousness or Source or God, and then the question is, who is it that can be jealous or envious?

If I do nothing, then hate, envy and jealousy need not ever arise.

There is no 'one' to be envious of.

And certainly no 'one' to hate!

Consciousness or God is all there is.

So, how could I be jealous of God?

The Unforgiven Sin

"Forgive them, for they know not what they do."—Jesus

This is what Jesus is supposed to have said. He was speaking to an audience that was still very much believing in sin and hell and damnation. However, perhaps what he meant was, *they* are really not doing anything, so forget about it!

Forgiveness as defined in the New Penguin English Dictionary is —*"to stop being resentful towards somebody"*.

So, who is this somebody?

Who is resentful and who is in need of forgiveness?

And who or what is it that is doing the forgiving?!

All are body-mind organisms acting out their programs.

Consciousness is all there is.

And, everything is interrelated to everything else.

There can't be any victims or perpetrators per se!

And, there is truly no 'one' to forgive!

Sin is described as—*"an offence against moral or religious law or Divine commandment,"* and is usually taken to refer to moral (and especially sexual) misconduct. The word 'sin' also implies a state in which a person has *chosen* to separate him/herself from God. Since breaking moral or religious rules is believed by some to be a sign of such separation, sin has come to refer more generally to the action, rather than the spiritual state.

If there is really no free will per se, and, no person per se, how could there be any sin per se?

And, knowing that Consciousness or God is all there is, then who or what is it that thinks he/she has chosen to separate from God?

This is the *Unforgiven Sin.*

The end of worry and disappointment

"Make no thoughts for the morrow for the morrow shall take care of itself"
—Jesus

With the acceptance that I am not the doer, the wanting, or hoping for things to get better in the future dissolves.

And, why worry about the future of a bmo that is already programmed?

Tomorrow will take care of Itself.

The way I see it, the only reason one is disappointed is because there has been some kind of expectation of the way something or someone is supposed to be or act, etc.

By understanding that everyone else is also programmed to do or act as they are.

And, that they are not the author of any action, all thoughts about the way things or people should or shouldn't be fall away as they arise.

Usually with a chuckle, or hearty laugh!

Freedom—Do whatever you want to do

Therefore, God's will need not prevent me from doing anything I think I should do, because He has done the programming.

In other words, the biggest freedom is: to be able to do whatever I like, whatever Bob *thinks* he should do with total conviction that never ever will I have to ask for God's forgiveness.

I will never ever have to ask for God's forgiveness for any action, for it is truly not *my* action. What more freedom can one want?

Ok. So, all this talk about destiny and doing whatever one wants. Do I mean throwing caution to the wind and running naked down Main Street or driving my car at crazy speeds without my seatbelt on, or sticking my tongue in a light socket to see what happens?

No, far from it! My programming won't let me do any of these things. Well maybe run naked… just kidding.

Ask yourself, if there were no laws against murder or rape or any of a number of so called crimes, would you go out and shoot people?

No.

And, why not?

Because, it is not your nature.

Where does your nature come from?

The answer is always the same—Consciousness is all there is.

Of course, all actions performed do have consequences.

The Devil made me do it!

"I've got a bone to pick with you young fella."—Dad

Oh, how I hated to hear those words. It usually meant that my father had discovered something I had done and that I was about to be chastised. Like the time when I was fourteen and he found out that I had been racing with the family car when I was supposed to be babysitting my younger brother and two sisters.

All actions do have consequences.

And, recently an incident happened whereby I did something that upset someone else. The action was basically my being negligent about monitoring the use of an electric heater. The other person was paying for the electricity, and being of a frugal nature, and not wanting to waste energy or money, this person was very upset. And, his nature was to be confrontational and express his anger towards me and this action.

Well, my nature is first of all to avoid confrontation and to be sensitive toward others, you know, like putting the toilet seat back down. Secondly, it is also my nature to be stubborn and not like to be told what to do. So, as these two natures came together over what at first glance seemed fairly insignificant, a drama was created (happened).

It was unsettling for me to have *caused* the other person any angst. However the other part of Bob's nature was telling a story of how silly it was for either of us to be upset over this issue.

And, over the next few hours there was much hilarity watching the ego have a field day making up all kinds of plausible excuses as to why I was right and how it wasn't 'my' fault, it was an innocent error, etc. etc. The bottom line here is that I knew that there would not be peace until an apology was made.

Again, all actions do have consequences!

But there is no reason to ask for God's forgiveness. Why should I, He's the one that created the drama in the first place.

There is no such thing as *personal* responsibility.

It's not *"The Devil made me do it,"* it's *"God made me do it!"*

And this is the *Cosmic Joke*.

Planning for Now

"All you really need to do is accept this moment fully. You are then at ease in the here and now and at ease with yourself."—Eckhart Tolle

The timeless dimension of Now is perpetual infinity.

The Now *is* Consciousness.

Consciousness is all there is.

And, therefore the Present Moment is all there is.

Nothing *happens* outside of Now.

The Now is outside of duration or time and therefore outside of now, but includes the present moment.

All sense perception is instantaneous and impersonal. But as soon as 'I' recognise an object perceived by 'me' the subject, intellection has taken place, and the present moment belongs to the past. The intellect only feeds on dead meat.

The Now is experience without an experiencer.

I used to think that I should not do any planning for the future and live only in the present moment. But Bob cannot *experience* the present moment.

However, what this 'understanding' has done is to allow me to accept whatever *happens.*

If planning for the future *happens.* So be it. It must be the will of the Source.

Acceptance doesn't necessarily mean approval or disapproval.

It simply means offering no resistance to whatever is happening now.

The 'why' question

The understanding is, that there is no definitive answer to the question," Why?"

And, in order to answer the question, "Why did such and such happen?", one would have to know the complete workings of the universe from the moment of conception or what is called the big bang.

In a universe where everything is interrelated and interconnected to everything else, no 'chance' events are possible.

God doesn't make mistakes.

There is no definitive single reason for anything *happening*.

There is no one thing causing something to *happen*.

The universe is infinite.

Infinity means no beginning or ending

In order for something to *happen* it would have to have a hypothetical starting and stopping point.

No such point exists in Infinity.

Therefore, in fact, there is nothing actually *happening*, only the *appearance* of change.

Calling and Purpose

"Accept whatever comes to you woven in the pattern of your destiny, for what could more aptly suit your needs"—Marcus Aurelius

When I was growing up I used to wonder what the future would bring. What would my occupation be, etc? My parents, always wanting the best for me, would be constantly encouraging me to stay in school, because for them, without a university degree I would have to struggle through life, and work at low paying jobs. But alas this was not to be—university or the low paying jobs that is.

Destiny had other plans for this bmo.

And, as I grew older I often thought about my/our purpose in this lifetime, especially at funerals, or when some perceived tragedy would happen.

The acceptance that I am an object which has been uniquely programmed by the Source to do whatever the Source wants, gives a brand new perspective on the age old question, "What is my calling?"

I now understand that whatever I am doing at any given moment IS my purpose.

The 'understanding' is that whatever is being done through 'me' at the present moment is my highest calling, and that the Present Moment is all there is.

Things are okay the way they are. I am not capable of exacting real change anyway.

And, if I could, what would I change?

What is, is. What isn't, is. And, what will be also is!

Consciousness, God, Source or Primal Energy is working, living, loving, laughing and crying, through this 'me' named Bob.

The Story of the Zen lamp

There is a story of a Zen master who grew up living with and listening to his venerable grandfather who was also a Zen master. When he was very young he often heard his grandfather say, *"Whatever is to happen will happen. Everything has a destined life."*

One day this boy, hurrying from here to there, knocked over a valuable and favourite vase belonging to his grandfather. The vase broke. So he went to his grandfather and said, *"You know that vase you like so much?" "Yes,"* the old gentleman replied. *"Well, its life ended three minutes ago."*

A Universal Problem

The working of the Universe has no problems.

The Universe goes on its mystical magical way until we start to observe it. And by observing it we create problems. The physicist, in observing, expects the universe to work in a particular way, according to common sense.

When he finds that the universe does not work according to common sense. And, when he discovers that a particle that was behaving like a particle, suddenly behaves like a wave. Then upon accepting the fact that it doesn't make sense, he invents a new name, 'wavicle'.

It is only in the act of observing and his *problem* with it not making sense, that he must create a solution by inventing a new name.

But the universe goes on its merry way. It has no problems.

Problems only arise when one observes.

So, 'I' create problems by saying, *"This should or shouldn't be."*

The only universal problem is the concept of the ego.

All so called problems dissolve when one accepts this fact!

Out of the wild blue yonder

"It came from out of the blue!"

I have heard this expression innumerable times.

People are usually referring to some insight or answer or idea that just popped into their heads.

It is usually unannounced and unexpected.

I think it's fairly obvious that the 'it' they are referring to is a thought.

But what is "the blue" they are talking about?

Is it particles of the sky falling into their awareness?

What is this "blue"?

Something to ponder.

Contemplating Meditation

"You are the world and the world is you. The understanding that the observer is the observed. And, to observe without the observer is true meditation."

—J. Krishnamurti

So, is meditation part of this understanding?

Perhaps most people think of meditation as quieting the mind.

For some it is sitting in a certain position, with the eyes closed trying to control or watch ones thoughts. And for others it is concentrating on one thing, a candle flame or reciting a mantra in order to get the mind to be quiet.

I think true meditation *happens* when there is awareness without thought.

When the doer is absent.

Therefore for me, true meditation can *happen* at any time with eyes open or closed. I cannot will it or make it happen.

And, as I sit here beside the ocean at Arbutus Cove 'contemplating' meditation, the sudden appearance of three dogs brings me back into the present and I am grateful for the interruption.

They put on quite a show!

Just witnessing them frolic and play in the water is meditation.

Then, in comes the 'great pretender' and starts to describe the scene, comparing, judging, liking or disliking, and the meditation is over.

Prayer

So, where does prayer come in?

Why should one assume that prayer is anything different than other forms of energy?

That intensity of desire, the intensity of wanting to do something is a kind of energy. To what extent this energy works, to what extent this energy produces results, one can't know.

So one prays for something, it happens, and we say, "My prayers have been answered." On the other hand, in many cases the prayers are not answered.

However, knowing that one is but an instrument of the Source, if prayer *happens*, one can just let it happen, knowing it is God's will.

The story of little Susie and God

When little Susie was about four years old she was an extremely restless child. At the end of the day her mother used to be thoroughly exhausted. So, one evening her mother said, *"Susie, look, you've completely worn me out. Now I'll give you a bath. Then after that I want you to go to your room, stay there quietly for five minutes and pray to God that He'll make you a better girl."*

So, Susie agreed and she went to her room and came out again after about two minutes. So her mother asked, *"Did you pray to God?"* She said, *"Yes mother I really prayed, because I really don't want to tire you, so I really prayed hard."* *"What did you pray for?"* asked the mother. Susie said, *"I did just what you asked. I prayed that He make me a better girl so I don't bother my mother so much. I really prayed hard."* So her mother was pleased.

But the next day, Susie being Susie, did all the same things again. So at the end of another long day, the mother asked, *"Susie, I thought you had prayed last night?"* She said, *"Mother I did pray, I prayed very hard. So if He has not made me a better girl, it means either He can do nothing about it or, He wants me to be as I am."*

Is God a vegetarian?

I would like to share a story from a David Hawkins talk in Sedona.

Someone in the audience asked Dr. Hawkins if it would be helpful to their spiritual evolution if they became a vegetarian. He smiled kindly at them and said, *"Well, you are meat."*

So, does the 'understanding' change one's normal living practices?

For instance, do you become a vegetarian, eat tofu, consume only organically grown products, grow a beard, shave your head, wear only hemp clothing or a loin cloth, live off the land, and sit on the front porch and watch the world go by?

No, on the contrary!

That is the real beauty of this 'understanding'—no changes are necessary!

If one eats meat or smokes or drinks or any number of what some people think of as less than righteous behaviour, so what, that is the way it is.

Besides, 'I' am not able to change anything anyway.

Life is being lived through 'me'.

If changes *happen* through this bmo, so be it.

It must be part of the Program.

Marvellous Diversity

"All that the human being can do is to wonder and marvel at the magnificence and variety of God's creation."—Meister Eckhart

Sitting here at my laptop, gazing out the window and waiting for more instructions, an occasional deer meanders by, almost close enough to touch and I marvel at he magnificence and variety of His creations!

Body/mind organisms are seen in the great Mystery with a sense of wonder that Consciousness could produce such diversity and yet be the same.

And, that God, Consciousness or Source, is immanent in billions of beings and yet each one is so diverse.

That no two human beings are alike. Even the finger prints are different, pulse rates are different, the voice graphs are different.

So, the understanding is that, in that diversity there is Oneness which is immanent.

Consciousness is all there is.

All there is, is the impersonal functioning of Consciousness, or God, reflecting within Itself the Totality of manifestation.

Gandhi vs. Bush

And, speaking of diversity.

I can think of no better comparison than Gandhi vs. Bush.

They epitomize power vs. force.

They are truly polar opposites when it comes to both their level of consciousness and their way of leading people.

However, I am reminded that they are both body-mind organisms.

And, they were both created and programmed by the Source.

They are both part of the functioning of Totality.

One is not better than the other.

They are both an aspect of God or Consciousness.

Consciousness is all there is.

Co-creation makes sense

"You are here to enable the Divine purpose of the Universe to unfold. That is how important you are!"—Eckhart Tolle

Co-creation really makes more sense when one has this 'understanding'. All there is is Consciousness. And, in order for Consciousness to experience Itself it must use an object to do so. We/you/I are the objects. I don't create anything or cause anything to happen.

Some people believe that they can create their reality. They sit and they imagine that they have a big income and a big income comes. They say, "I visualized a silver Mercedes. Look, I have a silver Mercedes."

But the reality which they *think* they produce *is* the basic illusion. They *think* that *their* mentation causes a certain appearance in Consciousness.

The brain is inert matter, and cannot create thoughts.

What the 'understanding' then is: if income or a car or whatever their goal was to create, gets created, that was all part of the Script anyway.

There is an old saying that there are three kinds of people in the world. Those who make things happen. Those who watch things happen. And, those that don't know what the hell is happening.

This bmo, 'me', spent most of his life *making things happen.*

In my former business career, I was a staunch advocate for all the personal development gurus: Tony Robbins, Zig Ziglar, Wayne Dyer and many others. My Bible was Stephen Covey's 7 Habits, and I practiced these principles religiously in my daily life. I remember when I was in my twenties, writing down what seemed like pretty lofty goals.

And, most of them did come to fruition.

My question now is, "Who was the author of those goals in the first place?"

And the answer is always the same.

Consciousness is all there is.

Personal un-development

"Your head is already in the tiger's mouth. There is no escape"

—*Ramana Maharshi*

There is no recollection of wanting to or trying to start this relentless searching!

It happened anyway!

Once I had exhausted the path of personal development and discovered that it was actually Consciousness that was doing the searching, the personal un-development really shifted into high gear.

With the understanding that I am not the doer, and that I am bestowed with the dubious gift of intellect/egoic mind; and the realisation that my new goal of enlightenment was not attainable, as there is no 'one' to become enlightened.

And, that Divine hypnosis has made me think I am in charge of my life, then the whole process took on a different dimension.

The searching morphed and shifted into a constant *watchfulness.*

With the watching comes the *witnessing* that there is a flow *happening* that includes this bmo, yet is somehow outside or beyond me at the same time. The *witnessing* occurs spontaneously without a 'me' as the witness.

There is a feeling of 'at-home-ness' that is impossible to put into words.

And, at the same time a sense of being of service to *Everything.*

There is no longer the thought of things spiritual and everything else. The understanding is that everything is spiritual!

Consciousness is all there is!

The I of the i —
insight, instinct, intuition and intention

Insight – *one's ability to discern the true and underlying nature of something.*

Instinct – *the largely inherent tendency for one to respond in a particular way, without reason.*

Intuition – *one's power to attain direct knowledge without rational thought or drawing of conclusions from evidence available.*

Intention – *one's determination to act in a certain way. One's resolve or will, concentrated on something or some purpose with a specific goal in mind.*

Now, the big question is, "Who is this 'one'?!"

Who is the author of the insight?

Is it really 'my' insight, 'my' intuition, 'my' instinct or 'my' intention?

The *Logic of God concept* is that the intuition, insight and instinct *happen* through an organism that thinks it is a 'me'. An organism, given a name, unique programming and DNA, in order to have the insights happen through it.

The brain is inert matter and cannot create thoughts or insights!

Yet the organism called 'me' also has an ego/thinking mind that pretends that 'I' am doing the action or thinking.

There is no 'one' to do or be instinctive.

The organism has already been programmed with certain instincts just like any other animal, which will react accordingly to certain stimulus.

And, of late, there has been a lot of talk and books written about the power of intention.

Of course, intention is powerful, and visualization and determination seem to bring about some pretty incredible results. That is a given.

However, one might ask what or who is it that is prompting the desire or intention in the first place?!

Consciousness or Source or God is all there is.

Life – a synchronistic, circumstantial, accidental coincidence

Synchronicity is defined in the dictionary as: The 'coincidence' in a person's life of two or more events which seem to be linked in significance, but which have no causal connection.

Circumstance is defined as: a condition or event that accompanies causes or determines another or the totality of such conditions or events.

Accident is defined as: an event that happens from unknown causes.

Coincidence comes from the root word coincide, which originally meant the coming together of two perfect angles. So, coincidence is not a chance happening. It is a perfect coming together of exactly the right circumstances or conditions, but without a *specific* cause.

Life doesn't 'just' happen. And there aren't any 'chance' events!

Part Two

A Divine Play

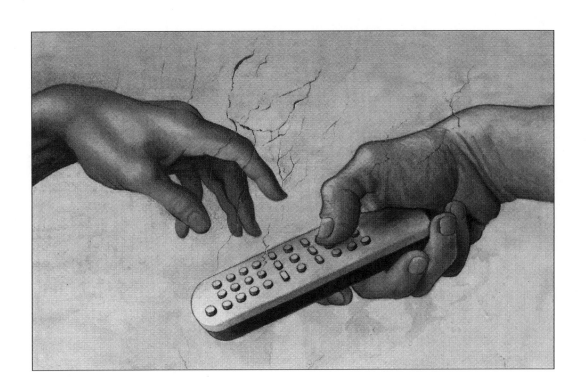

A Divine Play

Perhaps one can look at it as an unfinished, continuously ongoing play, movie or TV series. What is a play but a made-up story, an illusion created by a playwright or novelist.

The body/mind organisms function as characters in the Play.

Each bmo has been convinced to play a role in the Play and given certain characteristics so that certain actions, good, bad or indifferent, as society or the audience decides, will take place through that organism. As made up characters, where is the individual doer?

In life, or in this process of manifestation and its functioning, in order for this functioning to take place, for this Play to take place, for these love/hate relationships to arise, Consciousness has to identify Itself with an individual organism.

Now, suppose I write a play or a script for a movie. I create six characters, and I play all six characters. I become one character, and when I talk to another character the spotlight is on me as the character that is speaking. Then the light goes out for a moment and I become the other character. The spotlight goes back on and I talk like the second character. But who is talking? The other characters are not there.

I am acting different parts. It is still just me that is producing the play and playing all the characters. Reminds me of a movie character played by a young Leonardo DiCaprio, where he changes his identity and impersonates (now there is an interesting word) a number of characters, an airline pilot and a doctor among others.

That is precisely what is happening in this dream play. It is the intellect that makes those characters *think* that they are on their own and compare and judge one another. And Consciousness is just watching the fun in its objective expression as body/mind organisms acting out their roles.

Everything is preparation for the next scene!

Theatre of the Absurd

Once one *gets the joke,* the Cosmic Joke, that one *thinks* he has control of his/her life.

And, that 'I' think 'I' am able to make choices and effect change or direction of either my life or that of anyone else's.

Hilarity is the order of the day!

However, it can seem to be a tragic joke until the understanding begins.

But perhaps the most hilarity happens when one watches the antics of the ego, the 'great pretender', and its need to be constantly busy.

It continues to amaze me at some of the obscure memories that are brought up at the most unexpected times: playing background music tracks of favourite movies, CD's and oldie-goldie tunes from the past. And, the projection of and running of mental movies, replaying of past acts or events, rewriting of recent scenes to show 'me' in a more advantageous light, or running previews of possible future scenarios.

The mind surely replaces a lot of the film crew. It works as cameraman, editor, projectionist, soundman, and of course impersonating The Director.

It is truly the 'Theatre of the Absurd.'

Happy Days

Remember the TV sitcom 'Happy Days'? Well, during my adolescence I played the character of 'the Fonz', but my nick name was 'the Keeg'. I was really cool, man, and gave the impression of being a tough guy on the outside, but with a sensitive heart buried somewhere deep inside.

Although the Keeg didn't show a lot of emotion, he did have his ups and downs. When he asked the prettiest girl in school to go on a date, and she said yes, he acted way cool on the outside but was jumping for joy inside.

So, the big question I am sure is, "Does this understanding bring happiness?"

It might appear that getting the girl is what made the Keeg happy. The fact is that I was already a pretty happy guy. The joy was already on the inside just waiting for the right conditions to arise.

Anyway, back to the word (concept) of happiness.

Happiness is not the opposite of sadness. They are interrelated polarities.

One cannot make happiness *happen.* Happiness is an *arising* of joy from within.

It is experienced like a sliding scale or thermometer. At one end of the scale—there is elation and tears of joy, then to feeling great, to really good, good, then ok or fine, and then the other direction—sort of ok, fair to middling, not too good, bad, really bad, horrible, to utter despondency and tears of sadness.

Does the 'understanding' bring happiness?

The answer is, no, the understanding brings simplicity to life and if happiness or sadness *happen,* it is all part of the Play and I accept my part of the act. But, that doesn't mean I approve of the role, only that I trust the Producer.

I no longer look for anyone or anything to bring me happiness, and this attitude seems to allow a sense of peace within to *happen.*

All worry and anxiety about the future evaporates with the understanding that I am not the author, but an instrument through which Life happens.

Now, where did I put that comb?!

Me, myself and Irene

Just like Jim Carey in this hilarious spoof of dual personalities, when I watch myself in action, or when I (Bob) observe the observer (also Bob), it inevitably brings up a lot of questions.

Am I two people? And if so, who or what was it that was observing both of us?

Perhaps just like casting a shadow when I walk out in the sunlight, the 'other' Robert is really like a shadow of this body-mind complex I call myself. Or, am I just a shadow of Consciousness?

Maybe Consciousness is really like the light of the sun and we (Robert and I) are the shadow. But there can only be *one* shadow. Very confusing!!

And another thing.

When I talk to myself it is most often in the third person. In other words using the word *we* instead of I. For instance, *"We should get going; the ferry will be here soon!"* Or, using one of my other nicknames. Here is an example; *"What do you think Keeg, is that a beautiful woman or what?"* Of course this tends to be a one sided conversation, because the one asking the questions is the same one who is answering.

And, one more thing!

When I try to stop the continuous stream of conceptual thinking and non-stop noise in the head, it is always a fruitless waste of energy. Whether it be trying to stay in the 'I am' or conscious breathing, there is no way to stop it, at least not for very long. Again does that mean there are two of us, the thinker generating the thoughts, and the one trying to stop the thoughts?!

With the 'understanding' comes the realization that, the thinker and the thought, the voice in the head and the talker, the music and the DJ are all one and the same— the great pretender/ego/mind. The illusory 'me'.

There is no individual me or myself or Irene.

Consciousness is playing all these parts.

Now, that makes more sense to 'us' (Keeg and I).

Miracle on 34th Street

"Do you believe that your employee Kriss Kringle is really Santa Claus?"

That is the question the judge poses to department store owner R.H. Macy at Santa's trial in New York City just after the Thanksgiving Day Parade, in this 1947 classic.

To which Mr. Macy replies, *"Yes, your honour, I do! There are some things that you just have to believe in even if it doesn't make any common sense."*

Something the human mind cannot understand, or seems to have opposing meaning, is called a paradox.

In other cases it may be called a miracle.

Miracles are simply events which the human mind cannot explain with its existing knowledge.

Events *happen* in spite of human involvement, not because of it.

What is the significance of miracles? Nothing!

Things/events are created (miracles) so the pseudo-entities or bmo's (also miracles) will get further involved in the Play.

"Ho,Ho,Ho, and on with the show!"

Groundhog Day

This 1993 movie is destined to be a classic. Bill Murray 's a hoot as the surly, self-consumed weatherman, Phil, who has gone to a small town in Pennsylvania to cover the annual appearance or non-appearance of another Phil, the famous groundhog, Punxsutawney Phil.

Every day he keeps waking up at 6 am to the same song—Sonny and Cher singing "I've got you babe"—on his clock radio and proceeds to experience exactly the same day as he had experienced yesterday, over and over again!

Here is a short dialogue between Phil and Rita (Andie Mac Dowell), a news colleague whom Phil has been unsuccessfully trying to seduce. They are having coffee in the same restaurant he has been to everyday, for what must be many weeks by now.

Phil - *"I have something important to tell you."*

Rita - *"Oh, and what would that be?"*

Phil - *"I am God."*

Rita - *"What?!"*

Phil - *"Well, not THE God, but a god."*

Rita - *"No you are not God or a god! This is 12 years of Catholic school talking here!!"*

Just like Phil the weatherman, bmo's might predict what one will do or what might happen tomorrow or next week.

But just like the weather, it may or may not happen according to our prediction.

And, just like Phil the groundhog, 'I' might pop my head out to check for my shadow on a particular day in February, or maybe not.

And, even if Punxsutawney Phil does see his shadow, we may or may not have six more weeks of winter.

It all depends on Cosmic Law and the Divine Meteorologist.

The Meaning of Life

The Grim Reaper already has your number!

Anyone who has seen this classic Monte Python movie will recall the famous dinner scene at the end of the movie. The Grim Reaper knocks on the door and tells everyone they are now dead and to follow him. Someone asks, *"How could we all be dead?"* And the Grim Reaper points his skeleton finger at the dish on the table and growls, *"The salmon!"*

What if one knew that the exact time of one's death has already been programmed?

Of course 'I' am talking about the body/mind organism's death.

Wouldn't that knowledge bring a sigh of relief?

One would continue his/her life as before—there really is no choice. But, perhaps there would be a little less underlying anxiety about death and dying!

One thing is sure, if I had been at Monty Python's dinner table, I would not have eaten the salmon. God wouldn't let me. Unless of course it was written into the Script that this was my last supper!

So, what is the meaning of life?

Nothing!

The mind/intellect has been programmed from the beginning to believe that life is precious, life has a purpose, life has meaning.

Life has no meaning per se.

Nothing really matters (except to the ego).

Life happens!

Or, at least it appears to happen.

It is the Play of Consciousness.

Death of a Salesman

Here is an interesting quote from this Arthur Miller play—Biff says to his father (salesman Willy Loman), *"Pop, I'm a dime a dozen and so are you."*

Death of a salesman only becomes an issue if we consider ourselves a *'me',* and for a *'me'* this body/mind organism is the biggest thing to happen in the world.

Now, let us consider the concept of electricity. Nobody really knows exactly what electricity is. Electricity is what electricity does. Electricity thus is a concept, an aspect of Consciousness.

Electricity works through billions of tools and appliances. We can't see electricity, but we know its there. When Mr. Black & Decker or Ms. Fridgedare dies and gets demolished, what happens to the electricity?

The point is, when a body/mind organism dies the Consciousness which was functioning through that organism is precisely like the electricity functioning through the fridge or stove. If the appliance breaks, electricity continues to function.

For eons Bobs have been created and destroyed as part of the functioning of Totality, as part of God's will. How many billions of human organisms have been created and destroyed? Why do we attach importance to any one organism?

Because it is *'me',* Willy Loman, the salesman!

But when one sees it in perspective, body/mind organisms have been created and destroyed for thousands of years. What is the big deal when one bmo is destroyed?

The whole subjective illusion is that we/you/I *think* we are this body/mind, which causes us to worry what is going to happen to this *'me'* after the body dies.

When one understands that this *'me'* is only a concept, how can a concept be concerned with what happens after the body/mind is dead?

And besides, as the bartender was overheard saying to the rejected salesman drowning his sorrows in drink, "Cheer up old chap, women are like buses, another one will be along in a few minutes."

Karma and the Academy Awards

Karma is an old eastern term meaning action. Consciousness needs an object to produce certain actions. So it produces an object with certain characteristics that will produce precisely that action.

I have a certain computer program created for a certain purpose, so the moment the input goes in I know what the output will be. Consciousness, knowing the computer it has created, sends an input by way of a thought and knows precisely what the action is going to be. And those actions together with the actions of billions of others will make up the Totality of functioning at that moment.

Karma also means causality. It has nothing to do with the individual doer, the individual entity, because there *is no* individual entity as the doer. The *concept* of Karma is based on people being rewarded for doing 'good' deeds or punished for doing 'bad' deeds.

Good deeds *happen* through particular bmos and bad deeds *happen* through certain body/mind organisms. Both good deeds and bad deeds together form the functioning of Totality at that moment. It is only the human being who says 'good deeds, bad deeds'.

All are deeds performed, in this life and living by Consciousness, through bmos according to their natural characteristics. Some are labelled saints (Gandhi and Mother Theresa), others idiots and scoundrels (George W. Bush and Saddam Hussein).

A psychopath has not chosen to be a psychopath. Who has created the psychopath? He is part of the creation of the Totality of manifestation.

So, the concept is: certain acts take place. Those acts have consequences. The whole process is impersonal. No individual is guilty of anything. Certain acts *happen* through certain organisms and some get punished, and some get the Academy Award.

I Love Lucy

"Lucy, you got some splain'in to do!"—Ricky Ricardo

Perhaps you have seen some re-runs of this very successful 1950's TV comedy series. Cuban-born bandleader, Ricky Ricardo, and his wife, Lucy, live in a Brownstone apartment building on East 68th Street in New York City. The beautiful but daffy Lucy has the nasty habit of getting into jams, scrapes, and predicaments of all kinds. The Ricardos' best friends and landlords, Fred and Ethel Mertz, frequently find themselves in the middle of Lucy's outlandish escapades, whether she's plotting to land a part in her husband's nightclub act, determined to write her first novel, or concocting yet another sure-fire "get-rich-quick" scheme. And, of course, Ricky, upon discovering her latest, would confront Lucy with this famous expression. This Divine Play of life is acted out through each bmo as action and reaction. That is what keeps the drama going.

However, unlike Lucy, the consequences of an action do not necessarily affect the bmo that the action came through!

As an example, let us take the case of someone throwing a cigarette out the window and continuing to drive away, unaware that a huge forest fire has just been started.

Or from the famous trial of O. J. Simpson, "If the glove doesn't fit, you must acquit."

The consequences of an action may or may not affect or come back to this bmo.

It all depends on the Script.

Again, where is the *personal* responsibility!?

Consciousness is to blame for everything.

From Here to Eternity

The concept of reincarnation is Consciousness identifying itself with a separate ego each time a new organism is created.

The concept is that when the body dies, the bundle of thoughts, memories, and impressions all go into the pool of Consciousness.

For the subsequent functioning, certain actions or events must take place.

For those events to take place, new organisms are needed.

Organisms are created so that deeds can *happen*. Deeds are not created to punish or reward an organism. It is an inert organism that suddenly becomes conscious when there is sentience.

This continuity of different functions which have to be performed by different organisms is referred to as cause and effect.

Now listen to Buddha talking about reincarnation.

There is no statement which could be clearer.

He said, "As there is no self, there is no transmigration of self." Now, substitute 'soul' for self and you will read, "As there is no soul, there is no transmigration of soul".

But there are deeds and continued effects of deeds. There are deeds being done but no individual doer thereof. There is no entity that transmigrates; no self is transferred from one to another, but there is a voice uttered here and the echo of it comes back.

So this concept of reincarnation is: certain actions take place, and they have reactions. Call them ambitions not fulfilled, guilts about certain actions which have taken place.

All of it goes into the pool of Consciousness as bundles of energy from which it gets distributed to new organisms that are created. Then through these new organisms future deeds can take place.

People who remember 'past lives', are perhaps, actually remembering components or bundles from previous incarnations-- but not 'their' incarnation.

Deeds are taking place, but there is no individual doer.

All there is is Consciousness.

The Buddha doesn't lie!

Mr. Destiny

In this 1990 Fantasy/Comedy, Larry Burrows (James Belushi), is unhappy and feels powerless over his life. He believes his entire life could have turned out differently had he not struck out as the last batter in an important baseball game when a kid was. One night he meets this mysterious man, Mike the bartender (Michael Caine), who could change his fate by offering him that alternative life he always dreamed of. But as Burrows embarks on this journey of self discovery he realizes that even this new life has its problems and drawbacks..

Larry - *"I'm 35 years old, and my life is shit."*
Mike - *"Can't be all that bad."*
Larry - *"It's not that it's bad, you know, it's just that it's ordinary."*

Larry - *"So, Mike, do you do this a lot, I mean, you know, change peoples' lives and stuff?"*

Mike - *"I've been known to make a few adjustments now and again.*
Larry - *"How can my life change so much just because I hit one stinking baseball?"*

Mike - *"Well, you see Larry, one's destiny is a very complicated thing. Every incident in a person's life affects everything else that follows it. Instead of missing the baseball, however, you hit it. Then you became a hero, married the prom queen, and so on, and so forth, until you find yourself exactly where you are. So you see, hitting that baseball has spun your life off in an entirely new direction."*

Larry - *"Are you an angel or something?"*
Mike - *"Not exactly, no."*
Larry - *"Then what are you?"*

Mike - *"Have you ever been faced with a decision, and you weren't sure what to do?"*
Larry - *"Yeah, sure, plenty of times."*
Mike - *"And then something inside you made you choose one direction over another?"*
Larry - *"Yeah. So?"*

Mike - *"So that's me. I make the suggestions, and you make the choices. That's how destiny works, Larry - very subtly. Welcome to your new life, Larry. I hope you like it."*

This is a beautiful example of how the Script and Play work! The only thing that Michael neglected to mention was, that Larry only *thinks* he is making a choice.

Consciousness, or God or Primal Energy is the chooser!

And maybe He isn't very good at baseball.

Heaven Can Wait

For those who are stuck with the notion of heaven and hell and God as an entity 'out there' that punishes and rewards, or for those who believe in reincarnation, this Divine Play must be hell!

However, I am reminded that the only reason one is 'stuck' with any notion is that it is also His will.

I have met a few recovering Cathoholics and for them there seems to be a great deal to overcome in order to get to a place where they can at least begin to grasp some of the concepts presented here.

So, perhaps I was fortunate to have been born into a family where there was no formal religion and in fact the word God really never came up.

Although I did attend a few Sunday school services as a very young boy, mainly because the Calvary Baptist Church was right next door. The closest I came to any kind of regular religion was in public school, where we had to recite the Lord's Prayer each morning.

Maybe all that religious stuff was transcended in previous incarnations.

But, not 'my' incarnation!

(Thought you caught me eh?)

Soul Train

I think that the idea of there being a soul that *chooses* where it wants to be incarnated for the purpose of learning lessons is bullsh…!

First of all, 'souls'. The mind wants to create a concept. The mind knows that the body must die, but the mind, the *'me',* wants to live forever. If not in this body—of course it cannot in this body—then in some other body.

So the mind creates the concept of a soul moving from one body to another body. Or, if so inclined, from body to heaven or hell.

As Buddha said in a previous chapter, "There is no entity that transmigrates; no self is transferred from one to another."

All the bundles get brought together and their components are distributed, but not the same bundle, which could be the same as the 'soul'.

The concept of 'soul mates' is that the soul has split or separated. And, that there is another complimentary part of one's self somewhere 'out there'. And, that when 'I' reconnect with that other part 'I' will become whole again.

Ok, everyone knows how I feel about the notion of individual souls and soul travel.

I believe the word used was bull feces.

Having said that, past acting roles have brought the awareness that certain characters reflect back to 'me' an energy, or pattern of energy that makes 'me' *think* that some body/mind organisms are more special than others.

And, a lot of people have assigned the term 'soul mate' to their sweetheart or beloved.

I prefer to think of 'my' soul mate/sweetheart as the Beloved (well, most of the time).

The Beloved is not a noun; she is not an object, but rather the subject of the heart. She is a verb. She is *Beingness* constantly unfolding.

She is the Unnameable Immensity to which the homesick heart is drawn.

The Beloved is beyond experience, a constant possibility, a constant Presence.

I and the Beloved are One!

She is myself in a temporary expression.

Consciousness, God, Beloved or Universal Love, is all there is.

Sex and the City

It seems to me that this popular TV series is really about love/hate relationships. All of the characters, male and female are looking for Mr. or Ms. Right . Now, this is an area that Bob has excelled in. And, after many 'intimate' relationships he can tell you that sex plays only a very small, although seemingly significant role. However, in the beginning of the relationship, when one is 'in love' it usually means 'in lust' and sex and everything else about the 'other' is wonderful.

This is what is termed 'personal love' or *small 'L'* love.

The intensity of love from a personal point of view could lead to hatred and jealousy or even murder, because the mind says, 'I must have him or her' or 'she is "my" wife/girlfriend'. And perhaps after the conflict, if they haven't killed each other, back again to love. Luckily most love/hate relationships mutate into like/dislike relationships and the conflicts are a little less dramatic. Instead of killing one another perhaps we just ignore each other for a while until it becomes unbearable.

That is when the make-up sex gets the ball rolling again.

But, the intensity of love from a universal standpoint or *big 'L'* Love, could be that if he or she wants someone else, let him/her have them! That kind of intensity of love is one in which there is no personal purpose. The love, even as physical love, is of such intensity that it results in the ultimate sacrifice. The ultimate sacrifice is surrendering the 'me'.

Personal love and hate are interconnected polarities. We all want love without the hate. But, one cannot exist without the other.

Just knowing this might perhaps bring more understanding and less anxiety and conflict into relationships. Or at least reduce the severity of the swings between the polarities.

When 'understanding' at least begins, and one starts to realize that there is no doer, then it is accepted that the senses get attracted to their objects. The senses and their objects getting together is merely part of the 'act'. If the sex act *happens*, one can let it happen, why should I consider everything else God's will and not the sex act?

There is no reason to avoid sensual pleasure, no reason at all. When pleasure comes my way, I can accept it wholeheartedly, knowing that it is just pleasure, not 'my' pleasure. And, when it does not come my way, that is ok too!

When understanding deepens, there is gratitude for the present moment as the marvellous eternal moment, unrelated to time. And, there is uninhibited enjoyment of what the present moment has provided. Be it cream puffs or sex.

Gratitude arises.

Sometimes twice a night!

War of the Roses

The movie, "War of the Roses", can best be described as a slapstick tragedy concerning the decline and literal fall of a marriage. After 17 years, Oliver (Michael Douglas) and Barbara (Kathleen Turner) Rose want a divorce. Divorce lawyer Danny De Vito warns his prospective client that the story he's about to tell isn't a pretty one, but the client listens with eager intensity—as do the folks out there in the movie audience.

Now, for this couple there isn't anything resembling a "civilized agreement":

Barbara wants their opulent house, and Oliver isn't about to part with the domicile. Barbara nails the basement door shut while Oliver is downstairs, Oliver disrupts Barbara's fancy party by taking aim at the catered dinner, Barbara lays waste to Oliver's sports car....and so it goes, culminating in a disastrous showdown around, about and under the living room's fancy chandelier.

So, who or what is it that keeps these seemingly ludicrous and sometimes funny conflicts between spouses going? And what is fuelling the flames?!

Perhaps one sees the wife or husband as 'the other'. And, one doesn't really want the 'stuff', but doesn't want 'the other' to have it!

Once the 'Understanding' is part of one's life, then no person is seen as *the other*. Because there really is no *other*. All bmo's (including oneself) are recognized as only dream characters who are acting out the parts they have been programmed for.

And even while one may occasionally get caught up in identifying with these strong emotions that happen through us, and sometimes act in so called hateful or cruel ways, it really can't last for long.

Once I recognized the "Theatre of the Absurd" being acted out all around me, and that 'I' am both the dreamer and the dreamed characters in this Divine Play, the intensity of any emotion subsides and is usually laughed at!

And, there is absolutely no guilt associated with the actions, no matter how outrageous the action may have been. Regret maybe. But no guilt.

After all it wasn't the Devil that made me do it!

AND there isn't really a 'me' doing anything anyway!

Consciousness is all there is.

Romancing the Stone

This is a really fun, romantic movie, especially the mudslide scene with Michael Douglas and Kathleen Turner (again). Some might label this movie a 'chic flick.'

Anyway, this bmo, Bob, has been bestowed with a large portion of romanticism, and loves helping God experience romance. For 'me' there is just nothing quite like a candle-lit dinner, or a stroll on the beach at sunset with one's sweetie.

The knowing is, that I am only acting *as if'* the sweetie and I are lovers, when in fact, as part of the 'understanding' the sweetie is really the Sweetie or the Beloved. Rumi's poems are all written to God as the Beloved, and I think he really puts romance in its proper context. From the heart to the Heart!

Like This – By Rumi

In your light I learn to love.
In your beauty, how to make poems.
You dance inside my chest,
Where no one sees you.
But sometimes I do,
And that sight becomes my art.
If anyone asks you
how the perfect satisfaction
of all your sexual wanting
will look, lift your face
and say,
Like this.

If someone wants to know what "spirit" is,
or what "God's fragrance" means,
Lean your head toward him or her.
Keep your face there close.
Like this.

When someone quotes the old poetic image
about clouds gradually uncovering the moon,
slowly loosen knot by knot the strings of your robe.
Like this.

If anyone asks how Jesus raised the dead,
don't try to explain the miracle.
Kiss me on the lips.
Like this. Like this.
When lovers moan,
they're telling our story,
Like this.

When someone asks what it means
To "die for love", point
Here.

The Passion of Christ

Jesus the *"Prince of Peace",* was perhaps the ultimate expression of Love manifested as a human organism!

Love is *not* an emotion.

Emotion, like a thought or a desire, arises in the mind.

The arising of any thought or emotion or desire is always spontaneous. One cannot 'will' a particular emotion to arise nor can one keep it from arising. There is nothing one can 'do' about emotions arising. This is the basic understanding. It's a function of Consciousness.

Emotions may arise but they are not 'my' emotions.

There *is* love, there *is* compassion, there *is* humility, charity, whatever one calls it.

Love arises, compassion arises—but there is no *one* loving anything!

Each bmo is created with certain characteristics. Different organisms will attract different emotions, depending on their nature. No one is more loving than another or more compassionate than another.

Love and compassion *arise,* more or less, depending on the characteristics of the organism. It is completely impersonal!

And, just think, if all the characters were endowed with the same characteristics it would be a pretty dull play!

Married with Children

This was just given to me.

It was a question posed to a group of children.

They were asked, "How do people decide on whom to marry?"

Kristen aged 10 answers:

"No person really decides when they grow up who they are going to marry. God decides it all way before. And you get to find out later who you are stuck with."

Don't kids say the darndest things?!

Anger Management

Jack Nicholson and Adam Sandler team in this hilarious comedy. Adam plays Dave Buznik, a struggling junior executive with a pacifistic nature. But a simple misunderstanding aboard an airplane quickly escalates into a legal nightmare for Dave. Dr. Buddy Rydell (Jack), offers to treat Dave for his perceived anger problem when a judge is about to sentence him to prison.

Again, there is nothing one can 'do' about emotions arising.

This is the basic understanding. It's a function of Consciousness.

Emotions may arise but they are not 'my' emotions.

Anger may arise, but I am not angry. It is not 'my' anger.

Anger arises in Consciousness Itself, and is expressed through the instrument of bmo's.

Some organisms may be programmed to attract more anger than others, but they don't have any control over anger arising. It *happens* spontaneously.

Perhaps It even arose in Jesus when he encountered the money changers!

One cannot *manage* anger.

'I' may be able to suppress 'my' *reaction* to anger arising. However, I have no more control over anger than I do over breathing or those pesky little hairs that grow out of my nose!

Perhaps you have heard of the term 'emotional intelligence'? Well, this understanding could be called '*advanced* emotional intelligence'.

It allows 'me' to stop trying to control 'my' emotions and understand that it is impossibility anyway!

Understanding that everything is Consciousness or God, don't you think that anger or any other emotion would lose its intensity and fall away without making a 'big deal' out of it?

Don't you think this 'understanding' would bring more peace of mind, and a tendency to lighten up and laugh at oneself more often?

You bet!

Fear Factor

Is there such a thing as fear?

If one analyzes the word fear, perhaps one might see that there is no such thing as fear per se, only *fear of something*.

Fear is experienced only before or after an action. At the exact instant of an action happening, there is no fear. But, a split second later the brain reacts and the thinking mind (ego) takes over and brings up memories of some seemingly horrible or painful consequences based on the past. Or, perhaps projects possible scary future scenarios for 'us' to worry about.

There seems to be a lot of fear of something that *might* happen.

We are being constantly programmed by the media. Television newscasts are rife with reports of all kinds of scary stuff, including 'killer bees' (isn't that the name of a rock group?)

And, most television advertising is aimed at making 'us' feel fear of something.

We are constantly bombarded with ads that make 'us' fearful of just about everything—fear of getting or not getting something—the right job, girl or boyfriend, weight, good looks, money, the new car, the right house and on and on it goes. Or, fear of losing what we already have.

Perhaps if one just stops this ongoing programming, by switching off the news and tuning out the commercials, the fear of something that might happen may subside somewhat...

or maybe not.

And who is the 'us' that is fearful? *Us* is a fiction, an illusion, a concept. Body-mind organisms. Objects with a name and a story. There is no 'me' or 'you' or 'us'. No individual per se.

And, once one realizes that the bmo that the ego has identified with has been programmed from birth to death, and, that each organism has no control over either his/her actions or anyone else's, and certainly no control over what *might* happen next.

Then perhaps one will chill out, relax, and let life flow.

Remember that old saying, "**f**alse **e**vidence **a**ppearing **r**eal"?

Fear is a concept. Why be afraid of a concept?

Doesn't make any sense to us.

The Good the Bad and the Ugly

"Bobby, you have to take the good with the bad."—Mom

As a youngster, I remember Mom's words when I came home and things didn't seem to be going well in my life.

How profound those words turned out to be!

Of course 'I' have to take the good with the bad.

Good and bad are interrelated polarities. They are not opposites per se.

One can't have only what appears to be good, without its polarity of what appears to be bad.

Beauty cannot exist by itself. How would one know what beauty is unless there was its interrelated polarity of ugliness!

One cannot exist without the other.

Most bmo's want to experience one without the other. That cannot be done. And, all perceived suffering stems from not accepting this fact!

Life, or this Divine Play, is based on *duality*, or the play of opposites. However, when the ego/thinking mind gets 'involved', *dualism* is the result.

Dualism is the mental split between 'me' and 'other'.

And, as the ego/doer doesn't accept the natural functioning of duality—the interdependence of opposites— a conflict is created between the two members of a pair of perceived opposites, (good-bad, beauty-ugly, positive-negative, happy-unhappy, day-night, right-wrong, pleasure-pain, etc.) by 'wanting' or desiring one in the exclusion of the other,

The ego's endless pursuit of pleasure inevitably brings up its interrelated polarity, pain.

Nothing can be constant in life. Change is the very basis of life.

There is a famous Christian saying, *"This too shall pass"*.

Or, as the mantra of many Buddhists, *"The impermanence of all things"*.

When 'the understanding' began to deepen, whether it is happiness or misery, that understanding has brought about a tremendous change in perspective.

As the beauty of the countryside gives way to the ugliness of the city, 'I' might find myself saying, "That's a big so what Batman!"

A Kodak Moment

A famous ad from the 80's, "Capture a Kodak moment, use only Kodak film". Today seems pretty antiquated, what with the advent of digital cameras and cell phone cameras.

So, how come so many people take photos?

Perhaps just like the ad, 'to capture the moment'.

Most of us want to hang on to what we think of as pleasant experiences. So we take pictures and hope to capture the experience forever. But alas, this is impossible!

Experiences *happen* through each bmo only in the present moment. Then a split second later the mind/ego claims it as 'mine' and says that was a lovely experience or compares it with similar experiences, to judge whether or not this one is good or bad. And, whether or not to add it to the photo album in the mind.

All experience is impersonal.

There is no 'personal' experience.

'I' don't really experience anything!

Consciousness or Source or God is doing all the experiencing.

Consciousness is like the movie screen and we are the characters through which the Source is directing, producing and experiencing this play of Life.

Houston, we have a problem…
Uh-oh, better call Maaco!

The 'great pretender'(egoic mind) really cannot accept that it is not in charge and is constantly prodding me to believe that I *coulda, woulda or shoulda.*

And, by not accepting 'what is', problems are created.

It tries to persuade 'me' that 'I' could have done something differently, had 'I' had different information. This may or may not be true. But 'I' didn't have the information at the time that an action was taken!

This bmo reacted to a situation or thought according to it's programming, which is changing by the second and depends on new information, which is also part of the up-to-the moment programming.

And, there is no 'me' to react to any situation. Only this body-mind organism with a brain that is inert matter, which can only react according to its pre-established DNA and up-to-the moment programming.

Consciousness or God or Source, is all there is.

So, the next time 'I' have a dented fender 'I' won't make it into a problem, I'll just call Maaco.

Gone With the Wind

"Frankly Scarlett, who gives a damn?"—Rhett Butler

A 1939 American film classic in which a manipulative woman, Scarlett O'Hare (Vivien Leigh), and a roguish man, Rhett Butler (Clark Gable),carry on a turbulent love affair in the American south during the Civil War and Reconstruction.

Whenever I am anxious, angry, irritated, or feel an alignment with any number of emotions, it is always because I have identified and aligned those emotions with the ego/bmo/fictional character named Robert and think they are 'my' emotions.

The *understanding* brings with it a constant, relentless, watchfulness.

The question often arises "Who cares or gives a damn?"

So, who or what is it that cares?

Who or what is it that keeps the drama going?

There is no 'one' to respond to these questions!

Consciousness is all there is.

Forest Gump

"Life is like a box of chocolates, you never know what you're going to get."

—Forest...Forest Gump

And the picture diagram of what's inside each chocolate has been locked away in the Divine Vault, and only He holds the key.

Astrologers, clairvoyants and those with extraordinary psychic abilities have been predicting future events for years. Some have been fairly accurate, some have not.

Many Government leaders and other so called highly intelligent people are frequent users of Astrology and other means of predicting the future.

So, does this mean that most bmo's have a deep-down belief that things are *destined* to happen? And, that they really have no control over the future?

If so, what makes so many think they have any control over the present?

Doesn't make any sense to me.

As Good As It Gets

Ok, you guessed it, Jack Nicholson is one of 'my' favourite actors! In this 1997 comedy, Jack plays Melvin Udall, a cranky, bigoted, obsessive-compulsive writer, who finds his life turned upside down when neighbouring gay artist Simon (Greg Kinnear) is hospitalized and his dog is entrusted to Melvin. In addition, Carol (Helen Hunt), the only waitress who will tolerate him, must leave work to care for her sick son, making it impossible for Melvin to eat breakfast. A panic- stricken Jack barges in on his psychiatrist unannounced and upon leaving, asks the other patients sitting in the waiting room...

"What if this is as good as it gets?"

What a profound question!

Perhaps what one desperately wants is security.

One cannot be happy even if one gets whatever his/her heart desires.

He/she has a future to look forward to. However, his experience of the past tells him that change is the very essence of life, and that security has never had anything resembling permanency.

The result is that even against her better judgment she cannot help chasing this illusive thing called security, or something better than her present life situation.

When the 'understanding' begins to deepen, there is a joyous acceptance of the fact that there is no real security for a *concept*. And that Life is flowing through one's life like a continuously cascading river or stream.

When one truly understands that one is not the doer but instead is the river or stream, the desire for security falls away.

It is replaced by a much more powerful *knowing* that nothing can make one happy in the future.

One realizes that there is nothing to get.

And, no 'one' to do the getting.

And, that yes, this moment *is* as good as it gets!

It's ALL good. It's ALL GOD!

Consciousness is all there is.

The Magoo Factor

Remember the 1960's cartoon character Mr. Magoo?

Well, if you're too young, there was also a movie made in 1997 staring Leslie Nielson.

Mr. Magoo seemed to lead a charmed life. An older gentleman who appeared almost blind (he was actually nearsighted). He was constantly on the edge of disaster. He would be walking along the street when suddenly from above a piano being moved to an upper story window would break loose from its rope and be hurling down directly on top of him. Then, at the last second, he would casually stop to pick something up on the sidewalk and narrowly escape death for the umpteenth time.

Sometimes it *appears* that perhaps there is a behind the scenes helper to make sure 'I' stay the course and don't miss any of my lines or actions that have been written into the Script. This helper also seems to synchronize events happening and make sure other characters show up on cue.

Some people refer to them as guardian angels.

Who knows?

Or, *what* knows?

Of late I have been noticing things *happen* that are perhaps not as dramatic as Mr. Magoo's experiences, but elegantly subtle and becoming more and more frequent in their occurrences.

Or, perhaps it is just that I am much more aware of them.

It is usually a very simple thing like doing home repairs and the exact type of screw needed at the time shows up in my pocket.

And it usually brings a knowing smile to my face.

To Kill a Mockingbird

An American film classic, based upon a Pulitzer Prize-winning novel.

As long as I can remember I have been trying to kill two birds with one stone. And, sometimes three or four birds!

Efficiency, productivity, saving valuable time.

I have been taught (programmed) to believe that time is money, or if not money then something of value: such as being able to do something that is perceived to be more pleasurable than what I am doing in the present moment, or being paid for my time.

However, the 'understanding' really shines a spotlight on the illusion of time and how the ego uses me to make sure I am always out of time (the Now).

With the understanding that I am not the doer and that I am playing a part in the grandest of Plays, there is a dropping away of the urge to use time in the conventional sense.

This doesn't mean that I completely disregard clock time. On the contrary! Clock time is needed to function in this world. We need to catch an airplane or a ferry at a certain time, etc.

But what is one saving time for?

How can I possibly know what efficiency or productivity means?

In the total scheme of life's happenings everything is related to everything else and what appears to be wasteful or inefficient to one may be a wonderful gift to another.

The so-called tragic and senseless death of millions of humans in war is actually a bonanza to the micro organisms that help decompose the bodies.

These thoughts came to me while I was busy killing two birds. I was staining the front porch with the door open so the TV could be seen—the US Open golf tournament was on.

Women call this multi-tasking.

I call it my favourite 'pastime'—productive inefficiency!

The Legend of Bagger Vance

A great movie by Robert Redford, inspired by and loosely based on the Bhagavad-Gita.

Will Smith plays the part of the mystical caddie named Bagger Vance (Lord Krishna), and Matt Damon portrays the young, down and out golfer, Juna (Arjuna the warrior). Juna is playing a golf match against legendary golfers Walter Hagen and Bobby Jones and he is losing the battle. Bagger tells Juna to *"be one with the field."*

This is sometimes referred to as being in 'the zone' or 'in the flow'. Most accomplished artists, poets, musicians and athletes are very aware of 'the zone'.

With the 'understanding' that one is not the doer but is only an instrument through which Consciousness expresses Itself, surrender becomes much easier.

Golf is a sport that is dear to 'my' heart. And, I have had experiences of being in 'the zone' during a round of golf. When hitting the golf ball became effortless and the results seemed to be happening without 'me' doing anything.

I can recall an entire round of golf where I must have been in 'the flow' but didn't realize it until the end of the game. I was entertaining three of my best customers at my golf club. They were all contractors who rarely played golf and were unfamiliar with either how to play or some of the other nuances of the game, such as golf etiquette and slow play.

As they were my guests it was my responsibility to make sure they followed the rules of the club and all the unwritten do's and don'ts that most golfers live by, such as replacing divots and repairing ball marks, as well as keeping golf carts away from the greens, etc.

Well, I sure had my hands full with these guys!

It was a real challenge to keep them moving and not hold up play. I was busy running from one side of the fairway to the other to help them find their balls and repairing any damage to the course, while at the same time playing my own ball.

Anyway, we finally got finished and were socializing over a beverage or two in the clubhouse when one of the group who had been keeping score announced that I had carded a score of 70 or 2 under par!

This came as a complete surprise to me and I had to go over each hole again in my mind to make sure this was in fact correct. Well it was correct and I can only say that the thinking mind must have been so preoccupied that the game happened or 'flowed' and I ended up shooting my lowest score ever on this golf course!

Shell's Wonderful World of Golf

Shell's Wonderful World of Golf was a televised series of matches between two professional golfers that ran from 1962 to 2002. It started as a pre-recorded one hour program on Sunday afternoons and was notable for also including a lot of information about the host country for that weeks show. It also included the conversations between the contestants in between the shots. As such, it allowed to audience to feel they were part of a foursome traveling with the competitors and host as opposed to being just a spectator in the gallery.

I wanted to introduce a few comments from some of the most successful golfers in history about what goes on in their minds during the most complicated of all athletic actions - the golf swing.

Fred Couples, the all-time champion of the series says…

"As far as swing and techniques are concerned, I don't know diddly-squat. When I'm playing well I don't even take aim!"

From Jack Nicklaus in his book "Golf My Way". Jack was asked; *"How many swing thoughts do you have while addressing and hitting the golf ball?"*

Jack responds, *"Perhaps one or two. I must stress however, that no matter how many things you think about at address, you are, so to speak, merely programming the computer. Once you throw the switch the computer takes over! The golf swing 'happens' far too fast to consciously control your muscles."*

Tiger Woods when asked a similar question…

"From the time I walk up to the ball until I see it in the air, my mind is blank."

When the thinker/ego (Great Pretender) is absent, God or Source makes this game look like child's play!

The Accidental Tourist

"I've never seen a movie so sad in which there was so much genuine laughter. The Accidental Tourist is one of the best films of the year."—Roger Ebert

Sounds like a Cosmic Joke doesn't it?!

William Hurt plays a well-known travel advisor headquartered in Baltimore. The tragic death of his son causes him to withdraw from the world, which in turn prompts his wife (Kathleen Turner) to walk out on him. Discipline problems with his dead son's dog lead Hurt to hire flaky professional dogwalker/trainer played by Geena Davis (who won an Oscar for her performance).

Now, I realize that this is perhaps a poor segue into the topic of accidental happenings, but oh well, so be it, it seemed like a good idea at the time.

Recently I attended one of Wayne Liquorman's Talks—a weekend of teaching pure Advaita, here on Salt Spring Island. Wayne, a former businessman from California, spent many years with Ramesh Balsekar, and was instrumental in publishing some of Ramesh's books as well as his own gems including "Never Mind" (A journey into Non-Duality).

One of the attendees asked Wayne, "So, if I am not the author of any action, does that mean things just happen?" Upon which Wayne's eyes perked up and he growled, *"That's the problem, the word 'just'! Nothing just happens! That's the ego saying that if I didn't do it then it just happened!"*

Nothing *just* happens!

Nothing happens by chance. No mistakes are possible!

No random acts are possible. No random acts of violence (or kindness).

Everything happens by accident. Accident means 'no apparent cause'. Everything is an interrelated accident. There is not a specific cause for anything to happen.

And, it only *appears* to happen.

Oh, by the way, I picked-up a great bumper sticker at Wayne's talk; *"Pro-choicelessness".*

My word processor went crazy with that one!

Analyze this!

Billy Crystal plays a shrink (psychiatrist), who 'accidentally' gets hired by a mobster—played brilliantly by Robert De Niro—to help him overcome his anxieties and emotional problems.

Here are a few funny lines from the movie:

Robert – *"I wasn't really going to kill you."*

Billy – *"Yes you were!"*

Robert —*"Yeah…you're right, but I was feelin' conflicted about it."*

As was stated in the beginning of the book, *understanding* could be defined as; "the power to make experience intelligible by applying concepts.

So, the concept *"events happen, deeds are done but there is no individual doer thereof"* ,can only be made intelligible by applying this concept to one's own daily experiences.

Take a simple action: I am in a strange city and I end up eating at a unknown restaurant.

At the end of the day, if one analyzes the entire action as it happened, perhaps one might find that several thoughts came, over which there was no control.

A thought comes, "I'm hungry. I want to eat something. I don't have much money, so I want to find a clean restaurant where I will get reasonably good food at reasonably good prices." So I ask someone, "Is there a place…" "Sure just around the corner."

So, what happened? There were a series of thoughts. The brain responded to those thoughts according to circumstances over which I had no control.

At the end of the day, when one analyzes it, perhaps one might come to the conclusion that there was no control of any events or deeds. A thought occurred or one heard something, a suggestion, or saw something. The brain reacted to what was heard or seen or thought.

This analysis can be used for *any* action, and at the end of the day perhaps one will find from experience that it was not 'my' action!

Consciousness or God or Source has written the script and has been playing all the parts through the instruments just like Robert and Billy.

Bruce Almighty

The characters, played by bmo's Jim Carey and Morgan Freeman in

"Bruce Almighty", represent the paradox that humankind is faced with.

A God that is both immanent and transcendent.

Omniscient and omnipresent.

However, this paradox dissolves when one understands that Consciousness, Source or Primal Energy or God is all there is.

And, that everyone one meets is both Jim Carey and Morgan Freeman.

Everyone I meet is a temporary expression of God!

EVERYTHING is God.

And, NOTHING (no thing) is God.

Consciousness is all there is!

Back to the Future

Marty McFly (Michael J. Fox), a typical American teenager of the 80's, is accidentally sent back to 1955 in a plutonium-powered DeLorean "time machine" invented by slightly mad scientist, Doctor Emmet Brown (Christopher Lloyd). During his often hysterical, always amazing trip back in time, Marty must make certain his teenage parents-to-be meet and fall in love, so he can get back to the future

However, the future for Marty is not shaping up well. His family is dysfunctional, his schoolteacher, Mr. Strickland, is out to get him, his music is just too loud and the rest of the world doesn't care. Only with his girlfriend and Doc Brown, does he find the encouragement and excitement that he needs.

Here is some dialogue from this 1985 Action Comedy.

Doc– *"When this baby hits 88 miles per hour you're gonna see some serious shit."*
Marty – *"88 miles per hour!"*
Doc – *"The temporal displacement will occur at exactly 1:20am and zero seconds."*

Marty –*"Ah, Jesus Christ! Jesus Christ, Doc, you just disintegrated Einstein!"*
Doc – *"Calm down, Marty, I didn't disintegrate anything. The molecular structure of both   Einstein and the car are completely intact."*

Marty – *"Then where the hell are they?"*
Doc – *"The appropriate question is, when the hell are they? You see, Einstein has just become the world's first time-traveler! I sent him into the future. One minute into the future to be exact. And at precisely 1:21am and zero seconds, we shall catch up with him and the Time machine."*

The body/mind organism named Einstein was created so that the famous "Theory of Relativity" could be brought forth and explained. Whereby, as one approaches the speed of light, time slows down.

And, according to "Quantum Theory", in space-time, everything for which each of us constitutes the past, the present and the future has already happened, and is being discovered by the conceptual mind.

So, there really is no need for a machine to travel either backward or forward in time.

As Ramesh Balsekar is so fond of saying –*"the movie is already in the can!"*

Mr. Ed

The expression, *"It came right from the horses' mouth",* has often been used to infer that whatever is being said must be true. Now, I don't know about you, but the only horse I have heard speak is Mr. Ed.

This hilarious TV series ran from 1961 to 1966.

Settling into their first home, newlyweds Wilbur, and his wife Carol, discover a horse in the barn. A neighbour tells them that the horse is theirs, left to them by the previous owner. Unable to part with the animal, Wilber persuades Carol to let him keep it. Shortly after, while brushing the horse (named Mr. Ed), Wilbur learns that he possesses the ability to talk, and because Wilbur is the only person he likes well enough to talk to, he will speak only to him. Stories depict the misadventures that befall Wilbur as he struggles to conceal the fact that he owns a talking horse.

Most stories and information that are retold or interpreted are done so according to the teller's *version* of truth.

Consciousness research reveals that the capacity for the human mind to comprehend truth depends on each human organism's level of perception.

What is *perceived* as true at one level is seen as fallacious at a higher level.

In other words, what some believe is true, is horseshit to someone else.

Although the human mind likes to believe it is dedicated to truth, in reality, what it really seeks is confirmation of what it already believes or knows. The ego is innately prideful and does not welcome the revelation that much of its beliefs are really perceptual illusions.

"A horse is a horse is a horse of course,
unless of course, the horse of course,
is the famous Mr. Ed."

An Inconvenient Truth

This 2006 film basically consists of a tour of Al Gore's climate change speeches. It is, in essence, one long speech in various cities around the world. There are short but noticeable periods when the film tries to be a biography of Al Gore at the same time.

So, what is (capital T) Truth?

With reference again to Dr. David R. Hawkins's work mentioned earlier, Hawkins states…

"Truth or Consciousness is the unlimited, omnipresent, universal energy field, carrier wave, and reservoir of all information available in the universe. And, more importantly, Truth is the very essence and substrate of capacity to know or experience. It is the irreducible, primary quality of existence."

And might I add, "It" is not an it.

As evolution and the level of Truth advances, the ego is recognized as the illusion that it is and loses its strength, so that awareness of Truth is illuminated and allows a new *perception* of the world and what one understands to be true.

The 'understanding' is, that there is only one Truth.

Consciousness or Source or Universal Energy or Truth is all there is!

And, this is very inconvenient to the ego.

Hero

This movie stars Dustin Hoffman as Bernie, a lifelong loser. He's a small-time Chicago thief whose wife has thrown him out, whose son doesn't admire him, and whose future is a prison term, for receiving stolen goods. Then one night an airliner crashes right in front of him on a deserted road, and although he's no hero, Bernie is responsible for pushing the plane's emergency door open, and personally rescuing several passengers - including a TV newswoman played by Geena Davis.

If it hadn't been for this little guy, everybody might have died. But they live, while he disappears back into the rainy night.

The TV station offers a reward of a $1 million for the identity of "The Angel of Flight 104," and an imposter appears - a homeless drifter (Andy Garcia) who knows the right answers because he picked up the hitchhiking Hoffman and heard his story.

At the end of the movie Bernie is having a heart to heart conversation with his son Buddy about truth…

"You remember when I said how I was gonna explain about life, Buddy? Well the thing about life is, it gets weird. People are always talking about truth. Everybody always knows what the truth is, like it was toilet paper or somethin', and they got a supply in the closet. But what you learn, as you get older is, there ain't no truth. All there is is bullshit, pardon my vulgarity here. Layers of it. One layer of bullshit on top of another. And what you do in life like when you get older is, you pick the layer of bullshit that you prefer and that's your bullshit, so to speak."

There you have it. A street-smart answer to Dr. Hawkins calibrated levels of Consciousness.

The only thing I might add is, that as Dr. Hawkins points out, your level of Consciousness or Truth or Bullshit is already established at birth.

And, 'I' only think I'm doing the choosing.

Consciousness or Truth or Bullshit is all there is!

What the Bleep do we know?!

This 2004 movie was a breakthrough in bringing modern science and spirituality much closer together and has caused quite a stir. The concept of "Quantum Physics" presented in the movie, comes within a whisker of acknowledging the presence of a single unifying force in the universe. However, there is a underlying sense that the scientists in the film still think they are in control and that we are the subjects observing other objects. And, in fact one of these scientists goes on at length about how *his* thoughts create *his* day!

Once one travels deeper into 'the rabbit hole', one realizes that just like Bugs Bunny and Elmer Fudd, It's all a big cartoon, and we are being drawn on the Screen of Life by the Creator. And, that the Creator is not different or separate from me.

So, the question then is; "How do I know, or how does one even know that I know?"

The resolution of this dilemma of a description of knowingness or absolute truth requires a leap beyond the intellect (which can only know 'about' something), to the understanding that the only verifiable reality of knowingness is by virtue of 'being' it.

The Theory of Everything

Here is something that I found interesting. During Dr. Hawkins research, the following question was posed to Consciousness through Kinesiology:

"The Quantum Physics 'Theory of Everything' is true?"

And the answer was yes.

So, what is this 'Everything'?

Something to ponder.

City Slickers

This 1991 Western/Comedy stars Billy Chrystal as Mitch, a middle aged big-city radio ads salesman. He and his friends Ed and Phil are having a mid-life crisis. They decide the best birthday gift is to go on a two week holiday in the wild west driving cattle from New Mexico to Colorado. There they meet a tough, leather-faced cowboy named Curly (Jack Palance), who not only teaches them how to become real cowboys, but also one or two other things about life, in the open air of the west.

Here is a dialogue between Curly and Mitch...

Curly: *"Do you know what the secret of life is?"*
Curly: *"This."* (holds up one finger)
Mitch: *"Your finger? "*
Curly: *"One thing. Just one thing. You stick to that and the rest don't mean shit."*
Mitch: *"But, what is the 'one thing'?"*
Curly: (smiles)*"That's what you have to find out."*

Life is about 'one thing'.

Consciousness is all there is.

And again, It isn't a thing!

The secret of 'The Secret'

"If how-to's were enough, we'd all be rich, skinny and happy."
—Brian Klemmer

"The Secret" is a recent book and film based upon the belief that what we think about becomes our reality. The Law of Attraction and visualizing what one wants etc. It is a how-to to get something that we think will make us happy.

As Dr. Hawkins said in one of his talks, *"Most people pray for a new Ford."*

The 'understanding' is that there truly is no 'one' to be rich, or skinny or happy!

No individual person per se.

And, that if it is the destiny or script of the organism, then certain events will take place in this Divine Play, including getting the new Ford.

And, if as part of our act I am to use certain how-to's or meditate etc., then that too is the will of the Source and part of the Script.

'I' don't create thoughts.

Thoughts happen through this bmo.

Events happen, deeds are done, but there is no individual doer thereof.

Consciousness, or God or Source is all there is.

This is the secret of the Secret

Pulp Fiction

A 1995 Pseudo Dark Comedy, staring John Travolta, Bruce Willis, Samuel L. Jackson and Uma Thurman.

Quentin Tarantino, the director, is the Jerry Lee Lewis of cinema, a pounding performer who doesn't care if he tears up the piano, as long as everybody is rocking. His movie "Pulp Fiction" is a comedy about blood, guts, violence, strange sex, drugs, fixed fights, dead body disposal, leather freaks, and a wristwatch that makes a dark journey down through the generations.

Now, when I first saw this film, I had to turn it off. The blood and guts were too much for me to handle. I was really taking it seriously!

Perhaps many of us tend to take things seriously. Things like life and living!

Once it is realized that we are all dreamed characters in this Divine Play.

And, once one realizes that one is not the Dreamer.

How can this Drama be taken seriously?!

The Cosmic Joke is on 'me'.

'I' do nothing.

'I' create nothing.

 'I' am but an instrument through which the Play happens.

Consciousness has created this Pulp Fiction called life and living.

To 'me' this has become a very funny movie!

Ebony and Ivory

—Written By Paul McCartney—Performed by Paul McCartney & Stevie Wonder

"Ebony and Ivory,
Live together in perfect harmony,
Side by side on my piano keyboard
Oh Lord, why don't we?"

So the question is, *"How come we are not happy all the time?"*

It is common sense that one cannot expect to never have any kind of pain – physical, psychological or financial.

Knowing this, what keeps us from being happy or contented all the time?

If one analyzes this question, then one comes to one simple conclusion:

"I am not happy because the 'other' will not always do what I want him or her to do. And, it is totally impractical to expect the 'other' to do whatever I want him/her to do, so therefore it seems impossible to be happy all the time."

However, if one is able to accept that everything is a happening according to Cosmic or Universal Law and has been programmed and predetermined, and that how a happening affects whom or what – for better or worse – is also according to Cosmic Law, then it is clear that no one is responsible for the condition one finds oneself in. And therefore, no 'one' or 'other' need be blamed for any action!

The results are, first, one is constantly at peace with himself and in harmony with the other. And second, his/her mind is free from pride or arrogance for one's own 'good' actions, or guilt and shame over 'bad' actions. And, free from hatred towards anyone for the 'other's' actions.

Anger or fear may arise, but they no longer take 'me' over or continue to inflict any kind of lasting pain.

By accepting everything that happens (for better or worse), as the will of the Source or God. And not blaming anyone for whatever happens, neither oneself or anyone else – then, peace and harmony prevail.

"I am what I am."—**Popeye**

As Nisargadatta Maharaj points out in "I Am That", whatever I point at, whether it be a physical object or the sky, I am that! And, the pointer is not!

Consciousness is all there is.

So, how could I be different or separate from That?

However, when I introduce myself to another bmo, I usually say;

"Hi, I'm Bob."

Even though deep down I know there is really no such person as Bob per se.

It would sound pretty stupid if I said;

"Hi I don't really exist, but you can speak to this body/mind organism that people call Bob."

Bob has a genetic predisposition (programming).

Bob is a psycho/somatic organism with a functioning element that must stick to the Script.

And, Bob really likes spinach!

The Heart of Rock 'n Roll is still beating!

Ok, now, I understand that I am a programmed body/mind organism with unique characteristics, that is being directed by the Source to make His Play work.

And, that I, Robert Keegan really 'do' nothing. That I am not the architect of any doing. That I am not directing any activity. That I am but a dreamed character imbued with sentience and given a script to act out for the Source.

And, that He needs me to go about my life 'acting as if' I have free will and doing and saying whatever I think I should be doing or saying. Otherwise, I guess there wouldn't be any conviction or feeling behind the 'acting' and the audience may tire easily and leave the Play.

One of keys to this understanding is that the Consciousness needs me to 'act as if' I am in charge of the doing. Well, let me rephrase that. The Source doesn't really need or want anything – It *is* every-thing and no-thing. However, as Buddha was quoted earlier, there appears to be a karmic echo that needs to be expressed.

So, I am sitting here on the back deck, contemplating the ending of this book, and soaking up the early morning rays of a brand new day. In the distance just barely audible over the squawking sea gulls, I hear the sound of Bob Seger singing, "Old Time Rock 'n Roll". My heart begins to dance! And, I am truly grateful for the role I think I am playing.

A little while later, I ask myself, "What sort of character would be playing loud rock 'n roll music at this time of the morning?"

Then I begin to laugh!

That's a Wrap

Before my *discovery*, it was becoming difficult to carry on a so-called normal conversation. People seemed to either talk about nothing—the weather, sports, movies—or what has *happened* in the past, or shoulds and shouldn'ts. There was also a lot of why or how come questions asked. Most people wanted an explanation why something had happened. Some were concerned with the 'what if' question and liked to hypothesize about things that might happen.

Working as an Executive Leadership Coach, it became increasingly taxing to listen to this gibberish and try to only see the "Christ" in people.

However, now it is understood that it is not 'them' asking the dumb questions, and that they are but characters playing the parts they have been scripted for, and that Consciousness needs us to *act as if* something is happening.

Now, tolerance and compassion arise instead of irritation (usually). Listening has become effortless. After all, one never knows what is going to come out of God's mouth next!

This *discovery* has produced what can only be described as *a sense of relaxed freedom.*

And, when a 'why' question is asked, the simple answer is, "Why not?"

However, more often one might say, "Well, I guess it just wasn't in the program."

Look, this *Logic of God* concept is really quite simple.

We live in concepts.

We can say and *act as if* we are the architects of our lives, but deep down we know that is just another concept.

Take the concept of night and day. Day is not the opposite of night. They are conditions that *appear to happen* when the sun is either present or not. But they are not opposites. They are interrelated polarities.

We *act as if* and say the sun rises and sets. But we know that the earth is rotating around the sun.

So, as I sit here in the hot tub on a fine Salt Spring Island evening, enjoying watching the sun set over the ocean and dip down behind Mount Tuam, my heart is filled with gratitude and the thought comes…

"Yes! This is as good as it gets!" followed by… "and This!…and This!…and This!…"

The Final Curtain

This is Bob's *Swan Song* adapted from the lyrics of "My Way".
—written by Paul Anka and performed by Frank Sinatra, Elvis and others.

And now, the end is near
And so I face the final curtain,
My friend I'll say it clear
I'll state my case of which I'm certain,
I've lived a life that's full
I travelled each and every highway,
and more much more than this
I did it Thy way.

Regrets, I've had a few
But then again too few to mention,
I did what I had to do
And saw it through without exemption,
I planned each chartered course
Each careful step along the by-way,
And more, much more than this
I did it…Thy way.

Yes there were times I'm sure you knew
When I bit off more than I could chew,

But through it all when there was doubt
I ate it up and spit it out,
I faced it all and I stood tall
And did it…Thy way.

I've loved, I've laughed and cried
I've had my fill, my share of choosing,
And now, as tears subside,
I find it all so amusing,
To think, I did all that and may I say
In quite a shy way,
Oh yes, oh yes its true
I did it…Thy way.

For what is a man, what has he got,
If not Thyself then he has not,
To say the things he truly feels,
And all the words of one who kneels,
The record shows, I let It flow,
And… did… it… Thy way.

Elvis has left the building

There is a famous Zen Master's saying:

"Before enlightenment, chop wood and carry water. After enlightenment, chop wood and carry water."

So, what is this thing called enlightenment?

Enlightenment is an *event* in Consciousness, a very, rare event, but still an *event*.

According to Dr.David Hawkins' latest research documented in his book "Truth vs Falsehood", there are only 6 body-mind organisms living on the planet today *through which* this *event* has happened. That is rare indeed, 6 out of what, 6 or 7 billion?!

(Note – three of the six are on page 217 at the back of this book.)

The odds of winning the lottery or being struck by lightning are much better.

Eckhart Tolle says;

"Awakening is a shift in consciousness in which thinking and awareness separate. Enlightenment is to die before you die, and realise that there is no death."

Of course he means death of the ego or the false made 'me'. The illusory self.

Ramesh Balsekar's answer to this question is:

"When the apparent but illusory identity called a person has disappeared into the awareness of total potentiality that it is and has always been, this is called enlightenment."

"The only difference between me and the ordinary person is that the sense personal of doership has left! The thinking mind has vanished and become permanently silent. What remains is –the Peace that passeth all understanding."

And, Ramesh goes on to explain that it is only the conceptual ego/me that even wants to know what happens at enlightenment, because after the event there is truly no 'one' to ask the question and no need to know the answer.

Enlightenment means all concepts have ceased.

Enlightenment isn't something that happens 'to' anyone. It is an impersonal *event*. No person can become enlightened. The person is a fictional, made up character, given a name and unique programming.

Enlightenment simply means, Elvis has left the building… *permanently!*

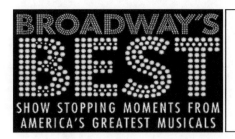

The Ultimate Understanding— There is nothing happening!

The Ultimate Understanding is there is no 'me' or 'Thee'.

All there is, is Consciousness projected as manifestation or form and Consciousness-at-rest when it is not projected, but they are not separate or united. There is only Unicity.

Nothing is happening and yet everything is happening!

Nothingness or no-thingness is spoken of as the potential energy. It is the potential which has activated itself in this manifestation. It is the unmanifest that has manifested itself. It is the subjectivity which has objectified itself. It is potential energy which has activated itself. That's all that has happened. They are not two states.

All there is, is Consciousness, at rest or in movement, but they are not separate states. Nothing has really happened. There is no creation. There is no destruction. There is no goal or path. There is no free will. There is no destiny.

Once this basic truth is understood with conviction, that nothing has happened and there is no creation, no destruction—then all that can happen is witnessing of whatever takes place through each body/mind organism as an appearance in this totality of appearances. And we can only witness it without questioning it. We can only witness 'what is'.

Consciousness, or Source, or God, or Primal Energy has produced this play.

Consciousness has written the script.

Consciousness is playing all the characters.

And Consciousness is witnessing the play.

It's a one man show.

It's a play of Consciousness.

You can remove the man and what remains is One,

Which is Unicity.

The Matrix vs. The Ultimate Understanding

This film evokes the Buddhist worldview with a smattering of Christianity thrown in.

Almost immediately after Neo is identified as 'the One', *"my own personal Jesus Christ,"* this appellation is given a distinctive Buddhist twist. The same hacker says: *"This never happened. You don't exist."*

From the stupa-like pods which encase humans in horrific mechanistic fields to Cypher's selfish desire for sensations and pleasures of the matrix, Buddhist teachings form a foundation for much of the film's plot and imagery.

The matrix is described by Morpheus as *"a prison for your mind."* It is a dependent 'construct', made up of the interlocking projections of billions of human beings who are unaware of the illusory nature of the reality in which they live and are completely dependent on the hardware (brain) attached to their bodies and the elaborate software programs created by A.I. (Source or God).

This 'construct' resembles the Buddhist idea of *samsara*, which teaches that the world in which we live our daily lives is constructed only from the sensory projections formulated from our own desires.

When Morpheus takes Neo into the 'construct' to teach him about the matrix, Neo learns that the way in which he had perceived himself in the matrix is nothing more than *"the mental projection of your digital self."*

The perceived 'real' world, which we associate with what we feel, smell, taste and see*, "is simply electrical signals interpreted by your brain." The world",* Morpheus explains, *"exists now only as part of a neural interactive simulation that we call the matrix."*

According to *The Matrix,* the conviction of reality based upon sensory experience, ignorance, and desire keeps humans locked in illusion until they are able to recognize the false nature of this reality and relinquish their mistaken sense of identity.

The only thing that I would add is, this relinquishment of their 'mistaken sense of identity', or Enlightenment, can only happen if it is written into the Script.

And, furthermore, *there is really nothing happening.*

This Divine Play just like *The Matrix,* is a construct of the mind.

In Reality, there is no creation, there is no destruction, there is no goal or path. There is no individual, there is no volition or free will and there is no destiny.

All there is is Consciousness at rest or in movement, which is Unicity.

Unicity

Unicity is an old English word that was used by mystic writer Wei Wu Wei.

Ramesh uses the word often in his teachings to indicate neither duality nor non-duality.

Duality and non-duality are often used to indicate the interconnected aspects of Consciousness—the interconnected polarities or perceived opposites.

The word "unity" presupposes duality. Or, the joining of two or more into one whole.

Unicity, however, indicates or points to the fact that the noumenal and phenomenal, or the unmanifest (or pure potentiality) and the manifest (potential energy actualized as form), are not separate states. They are not united or divided. They are one state.

Unicity though still a concept, gives the idea that there can never be two. All there can be is Consciousness.

Unicity or Consciousness brings about duality by identifying Itself with each individual being, so that this process of the observer and the object observed, this Divine Play, can go on.

So, play your part in the comedy, but don't identify with your role!

Life.

A Divine Cosmic Drama,
sometimes a comedy and
sometimes a tragedy.

A meaningless,
synchronistic, circumstantial,
accidental coincidence.

A tapestry

ever being woven spontaneously
in the Present Moment,
with a single thread...

Consciousness.

And…
as Lieutenant Columbo used to say,
"Just one more thing".
Remember…
you aren't what you drive.
In fact 'you' aren't even driving!

Major Contributions to Robert's Search for Truth
(or the input to his up-to-date programming)

Books

Title	Written through
The 7 Habits of Highly Effective People	*Stephen Covey*
The 8th Habit	*" "*
The Path of Least Resistance	*Robert Fritz*
Good To Great	*Jim Collins*
The Tipping Point	*Malcolm Gladwell*
As a Man Thinketh	*James Allen*
Think and Grow Rich	*Napoleon Hill*
The Science of Getting Rich	*Wallace D. Wattles*
See You At The Top	*Zig Ziglar*
The Leader's Handbook	*Peter R. Scholtes*
Personal Coaching for Results	*Lou Tice*
Developing the Leader Within	*John C. Maxwell*
The Strategic Enterprise	*Bill Bishop*
Being the Solution	*Dr. Darrel Rutherford*
If How-to's Were Enough	*Brian Klemmer*
Mach II With Your Hair on Fire	*Richard Brooke*
The Next Trillion	*Paul Zane Pilzer*
Happy Pocket Full of Money	*David Cameron*
It's a Challenge to Succeed	*Jim Rohn*
The Greatest Networker in the World	*John Milton Fogg*
Liberating the Corporate Soul	*Richard Barrett*
Raising a Giant	*Robert Crisp*
Rich Dad Poor Dad (Series 6 books)	*Robert Kiyosaki*
The Art of the Deal	*Donald Trump*
Atlas Shrugged	*Ayn Rand*
Spiritual Marketing	*Joe Vitale*
Seed Money in Action	*" "*

You Were Born Rich	*Bob Proctor*
Money and the Meaning of Life	*Jacob Needleman*
Building Wealth	*Lester Thurow*
What to Say When You Talk to Yourself	*Shad Helmstette*
The Magic of Believing	*Claude Bristol*
The Richest Man in Babylon	*" "*
The Grand Deception	*Ed Griffen*
The Children of the Matrix	*David Icke*
Children of the Law of One	*Jon Peniel*
- The Lost Teachings of Atlantis	
Six Questions That Can Change Your Life	*N. Nowinski*
The Learning Revolution	*Gordon Dryden / J. Vos*
Beyond Success	*Brian Biro*
Flawless	*Louis A. Tartaglia*
Living With Passion	*Peter L. Hirsch*
Why People Don't Buy Things	*Washburn / Wallace*
The Chemistry of Success	*Lark / Richards*
The One Minute Millionaire	*M. V. Hansen / Robert Allen*
The Idea Virus	*Seth Godin*
The New Professionals	*King / Robinson*
Heart to Heart	*Digarmo / Tartaglia*
The Dore Lectures on Mental Science (1909)	*Thomas Troward*
Mind Control Marketing	*Mark Joyner*
Motivation and Personality	*Abraham Maslow*
Analytical Psychology	*Carl Jung*
Clearing for The Millennium	*Albert Clayton Gaulden*
Infinite Self	*Stuart Wilde*
Inspire	*Lance Secretan*
Jonathan Livingston Seagull	*Richard Bach*
Illusions – Adventures of a Reluctant Messiah	*" "*
The Bridge Across Forever	*" "*
One	*" "*
LEAP! *A Journey to Personal Power*	*Jonathan Creaghan*
and Possibilities	
The Monk Who Sold His Ferrari	*Robin Sharma*
Dance of the Fallen Monk	*George Fowler*

Spiritual Numerology   *David J. Pritkin*

The FORCE Is With You   *Stephen Simon*
Mystical Movie Messages that inspire our lives

The Energy of Money – *a Spiritual Guide*   *Maria Nemeth*
        to Financial and Personal Fulfillment

From Aging to Saging   *Schachter-Shalomi*
The Addict and the Sage   *Alan Cohen*
From Self to Selfhood   *the Sufi Masters*

The Pygmalion Project   *Montgomery*
The Light Shall Set You Free   *M. McClune*
Meditation – From Thought to Action   *Alexander Simpkins*
The Invisible Partners   *Sanford*
Loving What Is   *Byron Katie*

Return to Love   *Marianne Williamson*

The Essential TAO   *Thomas Cleary*
- Tao Te Ching, Teachings of the Chuang Tzu

The Essential Rumi   *Coleman Barks*

You Can Have It All   *Arnold Patent*
The Journey   *"   "*
Money and Beyond   *"   "*

The Disappearance of the Universe   *Gary R. Renard*
Looking for God   *Stephen Sadler*

The Four Agreements   *Don Miguel Ruiz*
Mastery of Love   *"   "*

The Art of Spiritual Dreaming   *Harold Klemp*
No Ordinary Moments   *Dan Milman*
Finding Flow   *Csikszentminalhi*

The Awakening   *James Polisak*
Notes to Myself   *Hugh Prather*
Pay It Forward   *Catherine Ryan Hyde*

Conversations with God 1,2,3   *Neale Donald Walsch*

The Celestine Prophecy   *James Redfield*
The Tenth Insight   *"   "*

The Prayer of Jabez	*Bruce Wilkinson*
The Isaiah Effect	*Greg Braden*
The Prophet	*Kahill Gibran*
Golf and the Spirit	*M. Scott Peck*
Reality and Illusion	*Robert Perry*
Relationships as a Spiritual Journey	*" "*
The Seven Spiritual Laws of Success	*Deepak Chopra*
Manifest Your Destiny	*Dr. Wayne W. Dyer*
Your Erroneous Zones	*" " " "*
There is a Spiritual Solution to Every Problem	*" " " "*
The Power of Intention	*" " " "*
Power vs. Force	*Dr. David R. Hawkins*
Eye of The I	*" " " "*
"I"	*" " " "*
Truth vs. Falsehood	*" " " "*
The Power of Now	*Eckhart Tolle*
A New Earth	*" "*
Stillness Speaks	*" "*
Total Freedom	*J. Krishnamurti*
Questions and Answers	*" "*
The Bhagavad-Gita	*Geoffrey Parrinder*
The Zen Teachings of Huang Po	*John Blofeld*
Maharshi's Gospel	*Ramana Maharshi*
Consciousness Speaks	*Ramesh S. Balsekar*
Who Cares?!	*" " " "*
I Am That	*Nisargatta Maharaj*
Never Mind	*Wayne Liquorman*
Embracing the Beloved	*Stephen and Ondrea Levine*

Courses, Seminars and Coaching

Investment in Excellence — *Lou Tice*

Creating What Matters — *Robert Fritz*

Accessing Abundance — *Teresa Romaine*

Prosperity From the Inside Out — *Elyse Hope Killoran*

Unleash Your Personal Power — *Anthony Robbins*

Power vs. Force — *Dr. David R. Hawkins*

Possibilities Coaching Program – 12 Month Personal Coaching
—*by Jonathan D. Creaghan*

The 7 Habits of Highly Effective Leaders – Seminar plus 10 years of Practice
—*by Stephen Covey*

A Course In Miracles (ACIM) – 365 day Self-study Course in Spiritual Psychology
—*by Jesus Christ (?) through Helen Schucman and William Thetford*

Expect the Unexpected—3 days of talks and Teaching of Pure Advaita
—*by Wayne Liquorman*

The Three Mysticeers

Dr. David R. Hawkins is an internationally known spiritual teacher, author, and speaker on the subject of advanced spiritual states, consciousness research, and the Realization of the Presence of God as Self.

His published works, as well as recorded lectures, have been widely recognized as unique in that a very advanced state of spiritual awareness occurred in an individual with a scientific and clinical background who was later able to verbalize and explain the unusual phenomenon in a manner that is clear and comprehensible.

The transition from the normal ego state of mind to its elimination by the Presence is described in the trilogy "Power versus Force " (1995) which won praise even from Mother Theresa, "The Eye of the I" (2001), and "I" (2003).

Eckhart Tolle was born in Germany, where he spent the first thirteen years of his life. After graduating from the University of London, he was a research scholar and supervisor at Cambridge University.

When he was twenty-nine, a profound spiritual transformation virtually dissolved his old identity and radically changed the course of his life. The next few years were devoted to understanding, integrating and deepening that transformation, which marked the beginning of an intense inward journey.

Since it was first published in 1997, "The Power of Now" has already had an impact on the collective consciousness.

Ramesh S. Balsekar, a retired bank president, golfer, husband, and father doesn't fit the stereotype of an Indian guru— which may account for Ramesh Balsekar's enormous popularity. His background and education, combined with his profound spiritual studies, make him an ideal bridge between East and West,

Recognized as one of the foremost contemporary sages and considered a Master of pure Advaita around the world, Ramesh, who is married and a father of three children, is widely regarded as a 'householder' Guru. He elaborates his own concepts with those of his Guru Nisargadatta Maharaj, the Buddha, Ramana Maharshi, selected Hindu scriptures as well as the teachings of Taoist Masters and Wei Wu Wei. All serve as pointers to the Truth - The Ultimate Understanding.

And finally…

"What exactly has all this got to do with the price of eggs?!"

Copyright Permission

Bob was born into a respected middle class Canadian family, but not high enough in social status to make him proud.

Bob had a physical form well-admired for its perfection, but it was small enough to keep him humble.

His education was high enough to be most useful in life, but not high enough to make him proud.

He was a success in sports high enough to be satisfied, but not proud.

His business career was successful and high enough to be admired, but not high enough to make him arrogant.

He always had this deep feeling that everyone was doing the best that they could do and he never held a grudge against anyone.

He was given a wife and family for which he has always been eternally grateful, but was not spared some grief to remind him not to forget what life is all about, and to be always grateful for what he does have.

He had an adequate number of temptations in his way so that he did not become too critical of others who have to face their own temptations.

He was given a lot to show him how little is needed to be content and how much could be given away.

Finally, it occurred to him, if God were to design a life for Himself in phenomenality, could it have been much different from this one?

ISBN 142515640-1

9 781425 156404

Edwards Brothers Malloy
Oxnard, CA USA
March 22, 2013